Medicine of One
Living at the Center
~
Path of The Circle

Lomakayu

Edited by Patty Kay Hall
and
Anne Miller

2014
Circle Books
Cottonwood, AZ, USA

Medicine of One

Cover painting "Lomakayu in the Quiet One" by Patty Kay Hall
www.pattykayhall.com

Copyright © 2014 by Lomakayu
All rights reserved.
This book or any portion thereof may not be reproduced
or used in any manner whatsoever without the express
written permission of the author except for the use
of brief quotations in a book review.

Circle Books
www.medicineofone.com
email: Lomakayu@medicineofone.com

Printed in the United States of America
First Printing, 2014
ISBN-13: 978-1502342478

CONTENTS

Acknowledgements   v
Foreword
  Monique C. Grelot, PhD
    Forensic Psychologist   vii
Editor's Preface
  Patty Kay Hall   xi
Preface   xix

PART ONE: TRUTH
  Invitation   3
1. The Trail of Our Truth   9
2. The Circle Lives Within Us   15
3. The Spine of Your Life   21
4. Clear the Way   29
5. Thinking   35
6. Loss of Deep Listening   41
7. Nothing Gets Thrown Out of the Circle   47

PART TWO: ACTION
8. The Journey   57
9. The True Action of Self-Love   63
10. The True Sun   73
11. Freedom Through Compassion   79
12. Loving the Hungry Ghost   85
13. The Warrior and the Victim   91
14. Peace: How We Meet Our Losses   105

PART THREE: THE GREAT MYSTERY
15. I Don't Know   117
16. Surrender   123
17. Prayer and Faith   131
18. Flow   137
19. The Magic of Soul Medicine   143
20. Creativity is Married to the
    Spiritual Quest   155

Medicine of One

PART FOUR: CHOICE
   21. Choosing Harmlessness or Greed   167
   22. To Be the Circle   173
   23. The Path   181
   24. Earnest Commitment   185
   25. Courage and Patience   191

PART FIVE: HOME
   26. The Quiet One   201
      - *Desert Sky*   205
      - *Guru Tree*   206
      - *River of Bone*   208
      - *The River Breathes*   211
      - *Holy Being of the Wind*   213
      - *Circle of Sun*   217
      - *Walk In Beauty*   218
      - *The Quiet One of the Circle*   219

Tribute by Anne Miller   223
Glossary   225
Index   229
About the Author -
   - *Contacts and Resources*   235

**Each chapter has corresponding videos that will enhance your understanding and reading experience. They can all be viewed by going to www.medicineofone.com.

Acknowledgments

     This could easily be a very long list beginning before the beginning. I am going to keep it brief and in the immediacy of the writing of Medicine of One. I thank Sonia Ratto Ferrer for encouraging me to follow through with my initial forty pages. But my thanks for this book coming into its current form, I give to Patty Kay Hall, not only my main editor, but a provocateur as well who has brought forty humble pages into its current form. Without her unwavering help, support, suggestions and unrestrained commitment to excellence this book would not exist. Patty also contributed her great talent as an artist by gifting her watercolor painting of me for the front cover. I thank my sister, Anne, who brought in her gifts as a secondary editor and captured much we would have otherwise missed. Not only do I thank her for an eye for detail and great expenditure of time and energy, but for her ability to see in helpful ways that were different than Patty or I. Finally, I thank all masters of awakening and truth who have tread the earth, and the people who have come to me for help who have *helped me* bring forth Medicine of One. I thank you all.

Medicine of One

Foreword
By Dr. Monique C. Grelot, PhD

Lomakayu's personal journey gave birth to his book *Medicine of One* and introduces us to the principal questions of *the Circle of Life*. The candid, honest, and humanistic narrative of his experiences invites the reader to scrutinize their life without judgment, blame or excuses, but rather with compassion, courage and deep understanding of the mechanics of being. *Being* implies physical, emotional, mental and spiritual layers of existence and those layers are explored to guide us through the process of finding our *true* selves within the Circle of Life.

I am trained as a neuropsychologist, with a specialty in Forensic Psychology. I am also a profiler and critical incident responder. There has always been a hunger in me that could not be assuaged and I knew that science is but a complement to spirituality in the true sense of the word. We cannot have one without the other. Recently, I voraciously read the writings of the modern physicists who now acknowledge the existence of a Supreme Being/Force whose fabric holds the entire Universe together, including you and me.

Even though I am trained scientifically and analytically my main concern has always been with understanding the nature of reality in general. Most specifically to understand the collective and individual consciousness in order to glimpse a possible coherent *Whole*, which is never static or complete but rather an unending process and *unfoldment*.

Medicine of One

When my granddaughter Alysia died from an accidental overdose of prescription drugs and alcohol my world fell apart, and these questions about the true meaning of life were ignited with her loss. She had become involved with one of her professors, a man ten years her senior who had a painful history medicated by drugs, alcohol and younger women ... students. I suspect that she, like myself, wanted to help, to save him from his suffering. She was a gentle soul with a big heart.

The pain does not fade when a child dies. One feels *gutted*. The questions remained more insistent as time went on and other pains replaced the initial shock. I was looking for answers to these questions that were more than just promises and assurances given for comfort. I, like many, live in the quagmire of *reality dreams*, often missing the reality of the present moment. For many months the things I created and built were only models of illusions about reality and the salvation I prayed for. I also realized I needed someone to help me. Neuropsychology is my profession. There were certainly many colleagues in my own backyard who could have counseled me. But I needed something else; something that could bring me closer to a world of truth psychology was not able to touch, unless I sought a psychologist trained in Jungian doctrine, an almost impossible quest in the area I live in. I broadened my search beyond the boundary of possibilities previously considered.

Searching for someone to help me was a process mixed with hope and paranoia as I knew many charlatans claim to be your *savior*. I came across the website of a man named Lomakayu. I had seen his name many years ago, before Alysia's death, when I started coming to Arizona for professional conferences in Phoenix. The website enticed me to explore it further with its colors and narrative. The painting that serves as a background for the website beckons one to look beyond the clouds, beyond the foreground of majestic red rocks. It challenges one to stand naked in front of oneself and creation. The face of this man, carved from the stones of the desert and honed by the sun, confronted me. I knew then my quest had ended.

Foreword

It had been a year since Alysia died. It was time to act. I picked the phone up and called. I remember asking questions in a weak and trembling voice where fear had stripped me of any place to hold on. Lomakayu's voice came across the miles, from Arizona to DC, clear, strong and impeccable. His infectious laughter resonated in my ear, soothing the fear and tentativeness of my quest for the Truth. I kept reminding myself that the sweetest reward for the seeker is Truth. I was on the road to healing my grief, rage and fear.

I have since journeyed to Arizona several times on retreat with Lomakayu, and each time felt the peace and truth within me become freer of my survivalist walls. When he sent me the book he was working on, *Medicine of One*, I felt once again I was in his presence. It was as if, in the simple act of reading it, the walls built around what I had been seeking my whole life were crumbling away and I could sense the peace in which the answers to my deep questions were revealed.

The division between the thinking mind and the still mind, so aptly explained in *Medicine of One*, made me realize I used far too many internal monologues to validate or invalidate my emotions, be they good, bad, ugly or indifferent. I used my thinking mind to control and distance myself from them. Hence movement was needed to become unstuck and to bring those emotions to the surface, and to love and accept them ALL. The tragic realization is we often feel trapped in our circumstances, not realizing the door of our prison is wide open. We stand frozen in place and we are too afraid to step out into freedom and self-salvation. Lomakayu urges us to *clear the way* for our *soul's journey*, and free ourselves from our self-imposed prison with patience, compassion and love.

Each chapter offers a new insight into our personal journey and how lifelong patterns of feelings, thinking and behaving have robbed each of us of a *here and now* Circle of Life, of our own personal Circle. I, of course, have my favorite chapters and those strike a harmonious chord in my soul. Those chapters, which we want to avoid, will act as a catalyst in you and me, and cannot be ignored no matter what!

We can endeavor to read the *Medicine of One* once, ten or a hundred times and each time we will find something new

Medicine of One

as we progress on the journey. At each new turn in the search for the meaning of our existence lies a new discovery. I already knew we often function on automatic pilot mode to sustain our precarious identity. But here in the *Medicine of One* was a way to break the cycle. Each time I read through the circle of the book something I missed or avoided appeared. The hardest parts I had to accept are about *self-love*. I was raised Catholic and always thought self-love was a selfish proposition, fraught with arrogance and definitely not to be cultivated in one's life.

Medicine of One is the result of twenty years spent helping people *clear the way* to peace and truth. It guides us on a journey of the Soul that takes us outside the self-imposed, punishing, and destructive thoughts, feelings and behaviors that shape our lives. It is a journey of self-awareness, self-acceptance and most importantly self-love, so we may *experience* peace in a constantly changing world.

It is difficult to let go of blaming myself, and others, for Alysia's death. I am still walking the journey. But I am right on the brink of a defining moment. It will probably happen with a single phrase or paragraph from the book you hold in your hands as when Lomakayu says:

> *Finally, I stand in the river, sometimes in the sand, sometimes in the mud ... and sometimes on river-cooled rocks slippery with algae. The river breathes and my feet breathe. These feet of mine in dialogue with the earth have carried me into the arms of my grace. What is me is brought forth and sings in my bones through this dialogue and connection. Gently, my* **i**-*dentity that is linked to stories of pain is dissolved, as I let the earth hold me and deliver me into the truth of Who Am I.*

And from that moment on when I think of Alysia I will smile as if smelling the scent of my favorite flower.

Monique C. Grelot PhD
Forensic Psychologist/Professor of Psychology
Washington, DC
October, 2014

Editor's Preface
By Patty Kay Hall

Medicine of One is about a journey, a pilgrimage Lomakayu calls, "coming home to one's self." *Medicine of One* is the path - the way - within which the *self* intuitively seeks to rediscover and reconnect with parts of itself that have been lost, often times for reasons unknown. Recovering these lost parts are key components to our ability to experience joy, peace, freedom, and a fulfilling life. They make us feel *alive.*

When Lomakayu asked if I was interested in editing *Medicine of One*, I agreed in a heartbeat. Having done private retreats with him several times in the past, I was very aware of the potential of this book in assisting people who were at the stage of their lives in which they were seeking answers and greater awareness of the self.

Lomakayu uses the basic shape of the circle as a foundation for working with Medicine of One. In Sacred Geometry, the circle is a symbol of *Oneness*. Since the Circle is a major part of this book, I thought the first and most important thing I should do to fully understand the *Medicine of One* was to make a Circle I could conveniently use indoors. I wanted first hand experience testing the Circle's efficacy each time Lomakayu recommended a different way to use it. I felt the power of the outdoor Circles when I worked with him five years ago. They seemed magical in their peacefulness and I wanted the magic of the Circle to be present no matter where I used it. I made my own Circle out of a painter's drop cloth and then painted a symbol on it I had envisioned. As soon as I sat in my Circle the results were immediate, positive, and profound. I could feel that the *shape* of the Circle seemed to create a vortex, a container of focused energy within the limits of the Circle's boundaries. It created an oracle-like quality that connected me with my deeper knowing. Lomakayu beautifully captures this feeling in *The Circle Lives Within Us*:

> *There is a very subtle, powerful energy in these Circles in the desert as if there was something in the ground itself. It penetrates through your very bones, as if you were bathing in an atmosphere, a peace that has a kind of strength. The body responds by becoming supremely rooted without any effort.*

Early in the writing of *Medicine of One* I commented to Lomakayu to be mindful of the chapter titles he was choosing, because we would be invoking those same energies by the sheer focus of the topic. When we were working on a chapter I found myself immersed into the core energies of the chapter titles by way of real life incidents. I learned what he meant when he wrote in the *Invitation:*

> *Dare to break free of the prison your mind creates. For hell is the human mind from which there is no exit ~ no exit unless you stop believing what the mind thinks.*

With each chapter came a wise teaching and profound learning. It was as if I was experiencing a remote retreat with Lomakayu that wouldn't end ... but I was home and alone, not in Arizona. Each time a chapter threw me into what Lomakayu calls "spins," I would go to my Circle and let the spins of emotion and thought move. I regained my center and a new, greater, more peaceful level of awareness took its place. The main point is learning to work with these moments so they don't overrun you or rule your life. This is part of *the path* and the journey you begin with Chapter One.

Editor's Preface

Lomakayu chose topics and wrote about them in a way the reader can open the book and pick out a specific topic. Then he interspersed a few fun flashback stories that give us an idea of cultural influences and life experiences that were formative elements for a young man on the move working his way toward his spiritual path. The stories are fascinating because they give the reader the message that at *any time* we too can decide to get on our spiritual path. It's never too late. His stories show he grew up like we all did, finding our way through our unique path one adventure after another, one broken heart after another, and one triumph after another.

Lomakayu's writing invokes and demands a different way of reading and endeavoring to understand the material, and that is to NOT THINK. He invites you to walk in his world *with* him and *feel* your way through this journey. Listen to the language of a world where rules don't apply. Rules can change and destroy the energy of a message. The calling to faithfully share the wisdom being made known during the writing of this book superseded the man-made rules of grammar. The subtle differences that lie between the words we speak as language, and the words we hear when we *listen,* are beacons of illumination.

Listen carefully to what comes through as you read the words *between* the words. By allowing yourself to be receptive to his rhythm and delivery of speech in the written word, you may find it will connect you with a *knowing* about the material that supersedes an intellectual understanding.

The unspoken parts of language are the integral parts of communication that convey things that have no words: hand gestures, voice intonation and inflection, pauses, facial expressions, and sitting in the energy of the person who is speaking. Lomakayu is a master of all of these components as he delivers the mystical, soulful, inspired, and deeply connected spoken word. Translating these unspoken elements into the written word was a challenge.

In some respects his is a language of symbols like some of the earliest written languages. In these ancient languages, a symbol, or glyph, means more than one word. The written form of these symbols imparts the meaning of all the knowledge to the viewer. The symbols Lomakayu uses are made of words, but like a glyph, they represent a much larger body of meaning. You will find phrases such as *To be the Circle*, *Spine of your life*, and even *Medicine of One* throughout the book, which are just some of the symbols that ought to have a glyph of their own. Keep them in mind as you search for their meaning along your journey. The more you read and work with the material to integrate it into your life, the greater your understanding of the symbol will be.

Another stylistic element of Lomakayu's language is to use adjectives where we would normally use a noun and using a noun as a verb. He asks you to sit in the *empty* ... not the *emptiness*. In the *Invitation* he says:

> *I, too, must surrender to the **empty** without rushing to fill it. I am speaking of the **empty** when the feeling of home is shaken apart along with my identity ... the **empty** when my closest, constant companion dies ... the **empty** when I am disappointed in myself ... the **empty** knowing that no one can know my world of experience no matter how precisely I might try to share its detail of feeling ...*

When I began editing, at first I would correct his usage. He insisted *empty* was the right word despite it not being grammatically correct. When I tuned into what he was actually saying and put aside the grammatical rules drilled into me, I understood the space he was describing. His admirable insistence on being *true* to the message coming through always prevailed.

There was great effort in writing and editing this text to maintain a fine balance between his natural poetic and lyrical style and the necessity to convey a more direct explanation of some of the profoundly unique elements and concepts of his work. I wanted the reader to not only enjoy the beauty of the writing but also come away with a real understanding of what it means to be on the path of the Medicine of One.

Editor's Preface

Lomakayu's language is a language you have to *feel* and reminds me of learning to read Shakespeare. If you get too caught up in trying to understand the words, the grammar, and phrasing, the more difficult it will be to understand. But if you sit back and allow yourself to *feel* the beauty of the language, to be open to it, you will have a much deeper understanding of what is being said. One of the most poetic passages comes from *The Quiet One: The River Breathes:*

> *The cold mud between my toes ... the birds in winter trees ... the pulse of my heart ... a rhythm rhyming with the life force of my heart ... and this* I, *born from the dance of the elements. The River breathes and I breathe. I am the River. I am the flow.*

From the deep, quiet resonance of the Quiet One your body may even alternately respond to a more challenging chapter like *The Warrior and the Victim* with a twinge or a pain. Our bodies have their own consciousness and will signal you before your conscious mind is even aware something just hit a nerve. This is called a *trigger*. Somewhere in your body is a memory screaming for attention and it wants a voice. The energies, concepts, or topics in this book are very real, and they are powerful ~ this means the beautiful ones as well as the not so beautiful ones. It is easy to get caught up in them, to be run by them, and most importantly to be triggered by them.

The Medicine of One is a journey that can feel like a labyrinth. You begin the process in one moment, and with each word read you take one step forward on this path. It's a Circular path with little nooks and crannies, where you stop and pause for a moment to ponder something profound, all the while journeying toward the center of *you*. You will find parts of yourself scattered throughout the chapters. Along the way you will experience insights, stories, questions, teachings, and observations all leading to a greater understanding of not only the *self*, but of the self's *place* in the great Circle of One. In the chapter *The Journey*, Lomakayu urges:

Medicine of One

> *It's time to grab the thread of the true self, which guides us out of the maze of the survivalist mind, and transform the maze into a labyrinth whose inward spiraling brings us home to the center where both maze and labyrinth is now a simple Circle of One.*

When I sit in my Circle, I am more clear with my thinking and more able to listen to the voice of the universe ... of the *within* ... of the *self* ... of the source Lomakayu calls *the flow*. This is the dimension Lomakayu connects with when he is *Soul Dreaming*. It is there for all of us to connect with, yet he does it effortlessly. As you are reading, listen and you will realize he is speaking the words he is hearing from *the flow*. This will emerge often throughout the book but never so beautifully as in the chapter, *The Quiet One*, which metamorphoses the reader into a meditative, almost mystical journey of what seems to be a landscape until we realize it is about Oneness.

> *The land is full of songs. It sings to me as a grand symphony in its vastness and every secret little place holds a melody, all born from a single harmonic of the Quiet One. It teaches me in its silent singing. It's not something I hear with my ears. It comes from my heart as an organ of listening, whose very rhythm beats in the harmonic ocean. My body is just a cup dipped in this ocean, dripping with tears of individuality.*

I learned a huge lesson while walking this journey with Lomakayu. Being in the center is like being in the eye of the storm where there is calm. This is what sitting in the center of my Circle feels like. It is the calm. We can *choose* at any time to step into it ... or *out* of it. I learned to be more of a compassionate observer to the occasional chaotic moments and with conscious awareness let those moments spin on their own, without getting involved. This saved me numerous incidences of getting caught up in what felt like the *spokes* of the *spinning wheels*. It is like deciding *not* to step into the path of a

Editor's Preface

cyclone or waters of a whirlpool ... when you have the choice *not* to. Being able to consciously make this choice is a source of empowerment and brings a more balanced, calm, and centered element to my life. There is definitely power and affect in the Circle, with or without your conscious participation, but with conscious participation, the possibilities are endless.

The best I can describe the approach to reading this book is one day you happen to meet Lomakayu as he is leaving his house. You see a man who embodies the term *sage* in the ancient mystical traditions. His deep connection to the land is obvious, and he says, "I'm taking a journey and if you want to come along ... we'll talk." I have imagined in reading and working with *Medicine of One* that this someone is *me*. So off we go. Walking ... talking ... walking ... talking ... listening ... listening some more ... smiling ... crying ... spinning ... losing control ... stabilizing ... recovering ... walking ... being ... listening ... being ... being ... and at some point the undisturbed quiet sets in.

Patty Kay Hall, Editor
Waterford, CT
October 5, 2014

Medicine of One

Preface

Medicine of One is a Circle formed from many influences. It shares much with the predecessor of all religions and spiritual traditions ~ shamanism, an earth based spirituality. Shamanism is everywhere on the earth people have inhabited. It was born from the *First People* of these lands.

The land of my Circles is a land resonant with 12,000 years of human history. Before the Yavapai and Tonto Apache lived here, it was the ancient land of the Hopi. Slightly to the North are the Navajo, whose stories of the land and living at the center I also resonate with. The wisdom of all these *First Peoples* exudes from the land and joins with the Eastern traditions of Hinduism and Buddhism in my Circle, which also have their shamanic origins.

I pay homage to all wisdoms born from the earth in our search for meaning and truth. All of them inevitably base themselves in compassion. Compassion is the Circle of Medicine of One. I haven't *created* anything. I have *listened* to what vibrated with the sound of truth until these collected notes formed a song. You hold that song in your hands. May it strike a chord in you that helps you *come home to yourself*.

Medicine of One

Part One

TRUTH

Medicine of One

*When there is great truth to what you want,
there will be great truth to what you give.*

From *The Circle of Life*
Lomakayu

Invitation
*Wait no more. Refuse to be who
you are not ... and be who you are.*

My name is Lomakayu. It means ... *Everything Finished Well.* I live in the desert and the desert lives in me. I AM FOREVER, but one day this flesh and bone, blood and thought ... this *I* ... will return to the five elements. Death seems far away ... until it's close. I live as if this *far away* is always close at hand, and this *now* is the first and last moment. So I write this with the sense that when it's finished ... *I* am finished. I cannot tell you what *it* means. I can only tell you about this *now*, not the next *now*. It's simple. *I don't know.* That is the essence of the living ground we share: the ultimate mysterious *I don't know.* So please share this intimate bread of life with me.

Your story is mine. I am above no single one. On my path of the Medicine of One all the stories of humanity and individual *humanness* are mine. I invite you to do the same. Stand above no one. Let *everyone's story* be *your story* as movements in *the One that you are*, as the Circle of the earth, the sun, the moon, and the cycle of life; and that will be the end of the *stories of suffering,* for they move within you and *you are* what they move *in. You* are what a thought, an emotion, a physical gesture, a divine inspiration *moves* through. It's simple, your quiet, present *now* ... this *now* that I use the idea and the feeling of a Circle to lead you *to* ... is the Medicine of One.

I love being. I love the sky and the sun, the river and

the mountains, the canyons and the trees. I love red, yellow, black, blue, and the white that holds them all. I love all the animals and I have had many who were my dearest friends precede me in this return home. I loved them, I cared for them, and many of them died in my arms sometimes as my own act of mercy for them. Losing what I love is not easy, but I love being and being in this human form is a wondrous thing. It's a wondrous thing, but we do *lose* what we love and there is pain. You might ask, "How do I have a steady ground of peace in spite of loss, pain, and tragedy? How do I touch my infinite eternal self and still lovingly move through this sensuous world and enjoy it? How do I live in two worlds in the same moment?"

The desert scape goes from green to brown and back to green, from bright yellow flowers, to lavender, to white, to ... *empty*. I, too, must surrender to these seasonal changes, which have a cycle like the movement of the sun: a cycle, which is timely, but in a timeless way. I, too, must surrender to *the empty* without rushing in to fill it. I am speaking of *the empty* when the feeling of *home* is shaken apart along with my *identity* ... *the empty* when my closest, constant companion dies ... *the empty* when I am disappointed in myself ... *the empty* knowing that no one can know my world of experience no matter how precisely I might try to share its detail of feeling, no matter how many times they might smile and nod their head. Ah, *the empty* endlessness of our losses which if fully felt invokes the rain from the sky and transforms the barren winter into living spring. If we can relax and let life move through us, the waves of *empty* invoke their own fullness. Breathe out fully and breathing in fully is inevitable. This kind of breath is a Circle. This Circle of breath establishes our own self-compassion to that which moves within us.

The Medicine of One invokes the sacredness of a Circle in the same way that it has been used to symbolize God and to create sacred places of circular form throughout history in cultures all over the world. It invokes the Circle to embody the idea of Oneness as Circles within Circles on into infinity. Most importantly it invokes the spacious feeling of a Circle as a way to talk about your own quiet, compassionate presence that is this sacred *Oneness*. Even the word One begins with a Circle.

Invitation

Our pain, our history, our memories, our emotions, some constantly in reaction and others frozen, can stand in the way to this feeling of presence and connection. They become like the wall of a castle, which both fortifies us and imprisons us. This prison becomes our own separated world that nobody knows. In this separateness we are separated from our true self. We have allowed this wall of protection to *own* us. But we must own the heavy stones of our history as a big-hearted Circle. Life is honored, celebrated, and enjoyed. It is not a weigh station, an in-between state on the way to reality. Life moves within the one true reality that is embodied as the Circle.

The world is within us because the world is what we see, and what each of us sees is unique. It's unique because no one has the same past and experience. Even with two or more people who live through the same event, the inner experience can never be exactly the same. There are so many moments we all have, some subtle and some traumatic, where this movement of life is denied. We breathe in and hold our breath, as if gathering these moments in our hearts and bodies, where they sit like a weight waiting for our love, waiting for us to reverse the unconscious living of our life from a place of control and survival, and the conscious judgments and regrets we forcefully hold against ourselves.

Medicine of One is more like a path than a teaching, because in walking it you invoke the Guru within. As you walk it there must be the desire to live at the center of the peace that you are. In the journey to become free of all fears and desires, this one desire remains until it, too, vanishes effortlessly.

My purpose is to incite and inspire you to take this walk. Walk with me as I share what I have learned from the desert and the wisdom teachings of our world. Walk it not for a few months or years, but walk it as a way of life. As a way of life the Medicine of One is the path of self-love and compassion, a godly love that is the Circle. And as that Circle of life it is incapable of judgment. It's about your presence as an unmoving space that allows all movements.

In the end, your earnest commitment is to the path of your own truth. This truth is not about beliefs or ideas. It's about a knowing that is the experience of who you really are.

Medicine of One

So, as you walk your path let your beliefs serve you and fall away like autumn leaves in the wind that reveal the essential thrust of the tree, the essential thrust of you in this world.

Dare to break free of the prison your mind creates. For hell is the human mind from which there is no exit; no exit unless you stop believing what the mind thinks. Wait no more. Dare to be free, and be the compassionate Circle of One. Refuse to be who you are not ... and be who you are.

Invitation

Take a Moment ...

Put your mind in the soles of your feet and listen compassionately as each foot engages the earth. Keep listening and keep walking with me until you are effortlessly quiet, as if the sound of your walking echoes the sound of the sea and lulls you into quiet peace. Let it be effortless, gentle, enjoyable, this listening with your feet. Now let the quiet peace be what you are walking on, engaged with. Let your quiet peace commune with the ground of quiet peace. Let your being melt into the ground of being, and do nothing but sit down into it and stay there. Give up all believing and just sit there and be the unbelievable, the unthinkable, the indefinable.

Medicine of One

Chapter One

The Trail of Our Truth

There is a direct relationship between self-compassion and how you behave. What you are hateful of within yourself will find its way into your behavior in harmful ways.

Look behind you as if gazing all the way back to the beginning of you as a human consciously behaving in the world. If that trail of behavior is one unending flow of consistency radiant with truth, self-compassion and peace, then you don't need to read this book. For myself, this trail has breaks, like a lifeline in my hand seeking its *true north.*

Don't dwell on the breaks and inconsistencies; start with now. Start with knowing what the true action of self-love and compassion are. I say this because in my own looking back, those actions contrary to my current behavior, which are in alignment with the spine of my life, were the result of lacking true self-compassion.

I knew I was on a spiritual path in life as a teenager. I knew awareness was a key. Later the ability to be truly present was also a key. But until the Medicine of One began to flower, that awareness and presence lacked true self-compassion. I also call this *affectionate awareness*. Until I knew what affectionate awareness was I continued to behave, at times, without clear awareness of the consequence of my actions. Without affectionate awareness to my own *hungers, needs,* and *fears,* those feelings continued to seek fulfillment in the world even though I believed I was behaving truthfully with presence.

Many times, when out in the desert, I come upon a slew of beer cans and garbage thrown about almost intentionally. Often a soft thought lingers in the background that the effort to toss it is almost equal to the effort of taking it with you and disposing of it properly. Other than that thought, I don't get involved in the spin of judgment toward those who left this *trail* behind, for I remember myself as a very young man in my late teens. A friend and I rented a cottage on a lake before heading off to college. He had an Evinrude ski boat, which we used to water ski. I can clearly see him on a slalom ski with a six-pack of beer between his legs. I also remember us filling the empty beer cans with water and sinking them to the bottom of the lake. Is this any different than the cans I come upon now? Of course not. When I find this litter I just calmly walk around picking it up, perhaps as if I am retrieving those cans from the bottom of the lake. I am compassionate to my own young ignorance and so I am able to be compassionate to the ignorance of others without leaving my own emotional garbage of righteous anger behind. Later in this book I share a song with the lines:

> *I have walked in the drunkard's shoes*
> *And turned the dark to light*
> *I have died many times*
> *And been a ghost to myself in this life*
> *I'm a murderer and a thief*
> *With absolutely no belief*
> *And oh the pain of alienation*
> *Is like no other grief.*

The truth of these lines is to convey periods in my soul's history when I behaved harmfully. Even in this life I have behaved harmfully, harmful because my actions rippled into the world as an unbalancing force. Those actions were spawned from greed, control, manipulation, fear, and desire, but outright ignorance more than any other ... ignorance meaning an absence of awareness, a place of being oblivious to the consequences of my actions.

This was all many years ago as a young man long before the beginnings of Medicine of One. I was always on a spiritual path, but in those earlier years it lacked the sense of living at the center of the Circle of who I am and the ripple effect of that in the world. It lacked self-compassion.

There are people who think they've never done a harmful action in their lives. These people will usually be extremely judgmental of the actions of others, extremely judgmental of themselves, and consequently completely lacking in the true freedom born from self-compassion. They may behave according to a moral code so rigid the dark side may have to find its way into the world. Look in the mirror of intolerance and see within yourself what you cannot tolerate. Be willing to allow the whole world within the compassionate Circle of your presence.

The Medicine of One is born from my own imperfection, born from my own mistakes, ignorance, and errors. There is a behavioral trail from long ago which some may hold against me, I am sure, like small, unpaid debts from 40 or 50 years ago. I remember as a six year old stealing some bubble gum from a little store. Do I need to go back and pay for that bubble gum? Or any other occasion when I may have taken what was not mine?

The Medicine of One is about *now*. The way forward is about *now*. Your actions now can free you from this *karma,* but only if they are born from self-compassion rather than guilt. Guilt is a reflection of the unmoved within. Guilt becomes part of our *identity*. It shapes and colors the lens through which we see the world. Actions performed through guilt and shame *repeatedly* perpetuate self-hate.

There are times when in the honoring of an acknowledgement of a wrong we have committed, we must right that wrong, and sometimes in the admission of this wrong, we free ourselves from this story through the gesture of that admission. From that freedom we behave differently and our *lifeline* is altered. But many times these actions are so old and so remote they can't be *fixed* or *righted*. The people and the places are gone. Hopefully the harms we have caused are small when compared to the possibilities of great harm that can be done in the world.

As a species we can be very unforgiving. Consider the members of the Third Reich who were involved with the extermination of Jewish people in their youth, who functioned from unawareness and an identity that came from that Third Reich. What if a man involved in this extermination, who was 25 at that time, somehow, somewhere, discovered this self-compassion whose greatest focus would be the *agony of regret for his horrific actions of ignorance.* Now he is 88 years old behaving from self-compassion and compassion for all. Can he be forgiven? Is it possible that he is no longer that identity? If you were a jury and judge what would you do?

This book is dedicated to the imperfect within us. Invoke your perfect self-compassion to all the moments of regret. Be loving to the ignorance, manipulation, needs, and fears, and in that action of true self-love free yourself to behave as the demonstration of this compassion in the world.

We move through the world as a body, a body of thought with a name. Many numbers are associated with that name, from our ages to our addresses, all accumulating as an identity. As a person of *identity*, we have challenges that threaten this identity, threaten its value, threaten its safety, and threaten its power. These threats are seen through the lens of our history of experience and define our behavior.

In this world, what is important is how we *behave*, not what we *profess to believe*, not a body of moral thoughts we call religion which become religion's rule book. Religions cling to an identity; and this is their great error. That identity is a worldview they must protect as the one and only truth. Christ was a demonstration of how to *behave*. If the kingdom of heaven is *within*, if this is the truth, this *within* is one and the same for all, and identity will block the way, for the way is through the door of *no* identity.

It is difficult to live in this world if we hold on too tightly to this identity. Identity is a thing of thought, belief, memory, and mind turned outward to the world of objects.

The Trail of Our Truth

When you think, you are always thinking about some *thing*, even if it's an idea, a memory, or a dream. The *thing* is not always solid.

I think *I* own many things, but *I* own nothing. What *I* think *I* own, as the cliché goes, can own *me*. But more importantly, the rejected emotional experiences of my soul can own and define my *identity*, since they create the unique lens through which *I* view *my* world. That perception is *the source that creates my behavior in defense of this identity.* Our relationship to this construct of identity is the prime determining factor of our behavior. Our behavior in the world, our actions, and our way of being are what we leave behind ~ *the trail of our truth.*

How we *behave*, how we live each day, how we move through the world, what our actions demonstrate to others as the truth of this life is the *trail of truth* we leave behind. Do we want to live a life that builds a tower of identity, and then devote our lives to its defense?

Behavior. What do I think? What do I speak? What is the true intent beneath my actions?

What I have said, we can know. We can believe it's truth. We can understand, but how can we truly be free of this hard thing called identity? Information spurs us forward but it will not free us from the prison made out of the stones of unmoved life and the mortar of thought and belief. This prison is made from the *solidity* of our stories. How to be *free*? How do I change my behavior?

I've had many people with children come to me who greatly regret their behavior with their children. When they look back at that *trail*, and now see their child moving into adulthood with their current awareness, there is regret. Or it may be right now in the present they find themselves exploding with anger at times that is harmful. They want to change this behavior but it keeps happening. Maybe as a child they grew up in an abusive, unpredictable, chaotic world, which created a great need for order and control. Children are children. They can be loud, rough, unaware, self-centered, and uncontrollable. Parents who want to change their behavior are trying to impose the same force on themselves they are imposing on their children. What they really want is to control their own behavior.

If you change your behavior through a force of will without showing self-compassion for that dark and hidden place within yourself that is driving that behavior, you set yourself up to create tension. You cast the *unwanted* further into the darkness. Self-compassion for the unmoved pain in your own childhood is the key to altering the path of behavior with your own children.

If somewhere, within the flow of these words, something incites you to the *true action* of self-love then my gratitude will shine. For the driving force through all of this is an incitement to live as the *truth that you are*, achieved by the *true action* of love, first toward your personal humanity and *Self* and then radiantly shared from that *Sun that you are* to the world. This is the alignment with the *spine of your life* from which flows your behavior into the world.

Chapter Two

The Circle Lives Within Us

There are many movements in this Circle ... But never forget that you are what they move in.

Twenty-five years ago I entered the Verde Valley through a gateway of rusty red rhyolite rock above the little mining town of Jerome, Arizona. Far in the distance, the San Francisco Peaks stood at 13,000 feet, capped with white snow. The Peaks are the home of the Kachina spirits of the Hopi. Below the Peaks, forming the southwest edge of the Colorado Plateau, known as the Mogollon Rim, were thousand foot high cliffs of bone white and red sandstones. All this was beneath the great Circle of the sky. Here in this place where I stood was the experience of vast spaciousness filled with the colors of rocks, sky, and clouds pregnant with moisture. The wind blew the clouds into different shapes, and depending on the elevation and wind force, they floated as solid masses or were breathed out from some godly force like plumes of sacred smoke cast over the valley. Here was the fifth element of spaciousness, the great Circle of the valley allowing all the other elements of fire, air, earth, and water to move.

I was standing on Mingus Mountain, known by the Yavapai Apache as Blue Mountain Flat On Top. I moved to that little mining town to dwell in the experience of spaciousness, not knowing then that here was the seed of the path of the Circle, the Medicine of One. Like a bird finding its way home by sensing magnetic north, an inner compass had brought me into the *Great Mysterious Circle*.

Medicine of One

It's so simple, the Circle. Even today with our vast scientific knowledge we experience the wonders of roundness with awe as we gaze at the moon, the sun, or the encircling horizon as we stand on a mountain top feeling as if we are at the center of the world. To the ancients the sun was a perfect sphere made of energy that allowed life to flourish on the earth; it was also the great creator of the known world. Perfect roundness is a kind of perfection and when viewed in the sky is a great wonder.

Today, off in the distance in a canyon that slices up through the Plateau, a fire is burning. The smoke billows straight up and is then dragged northwest by the wind. This fire could destroy homes and lives. As the sun sets it glows like a phoenix rising from the fire. How do we move through a life that has pain, death, destruction, and loss? The answer in the Medicine of One is *to be the Circle* to all that moves within it.

The Circle is the feeling of soft, relaxed, spacious breathing, and an unthinking presence, which are like the sky that everything moves in. Unconditional love and compassion are the essence of you as the Circle. This Circle can embody all religions in their essence, openness, compassion, and non-judgment. Quiet, unmoving, unthinking, uninvolved, yet present in everything ~ omnipresent. God *is* the Circle.

I build Circles. Circles of stone. My first Circle was built in that rusty red rhyolite that framed my entranceway into the Circle of the Valley below, which would become my home. This Circle still looms above the Valley undisturbed. It's been there for almost twenty years. In this Circle are bone white rocks brought from an area known as *Skeleton Bone*. This Circle is filled with the element of fire, which reaches to the sky above and it needed the anchoring of bone. Below in the valley, there are many Circles, some are on the Verde River and others on mesas aligning with pyramids in the distance, or sacred buttes. I walk the land to divine the spot and the *place* tells me, as I work on it, what form the Circle will take. Sometimes there are formations in the distance I want the Circle to align with, but I never decide the form of the Circle in advance. They are anchored in the land that anchors them in the earth and the universe and beyond. They are doorways to the beyond that is

The Circle Lives Within Us

you, where there is no inside or outside. As that doorway, it's as if some energetic force enters from an invisible world.

The universe of the Navajo is anchored by the four sacred mountains in each of the four directions. Twelve thousand years ago the Navajo began their migration to this land and anchored that universe in other locations on their way to their present home. Once here in the Southwest they established themselves at what they believed was the center of the world. My Circles, too, are anchored in the land that surrounds them.

There is a very subtle, powerful energy in these Circles in the desert as if there was something in the ground itself. It penetrates through your very bones, as if you were bathing in an atmosphere of peace, a peace that has a kind of strength. The body responds by becoming supremely rooted without any effort. Using kinesiology muscle testing you can test the body's change in energy and strength. As you move closer and closer to the Circle, you become stronger effortlessly. Only recently I have found that this energy expands outward from the Circle. I did not orchestrate any of this. It has happened without intent through the exchange between the natural powers of the spot, my quiet presence, and the presence of others.

I sit, I stand, and I lie in these Circles and bring my little **i**'s world of thinking, worry, and identity and give them all to this Circle, this earth, in a sigh of surrender. In this sigh of surrender my little **i** - with the dot of my mind atop the line of my body - unifies and becomes the big **I** that joins heaven and earth. I then give this still finite **I** to the infinite unknown. I surrender my *personal quiet* to the *greater quiet:* the infinite east and the infinite west, the infinite south and the infinite north. The directions are within me and like a pebble dropped in a pool of water, these Circles within Circles travel beyond time and space to the *no-thing*. This happens when you ... *Be the quiet.* When you think ... when thought moves ... the Circles fall back in on themselves, to the beginning Circle which is *you* sitting there thinking. Thinking is a movement in the Circle of *you*. Emotions move, the body moves, thoughts move, but you are the still Circle they move *in*. You are the *One* in which the limitless duality of thought and this world move.

Medicine of One

Ultimately the physical Circle is an aid to take you into the Circle of the self, a quiet presence that can be more easily surrendered to here in the quiet vastness than it would be sitting in front of your computer at home. We get so used to gross forms of stimuli; the quiet medicine of our essence is seldom felt beneath this constant hum of busyness.

A Circle drawn on the ground has an obvious center. The stone Circles, very specifically placed on the land, also have an obvious center. What does it mean to *be* this center, to abide in it, to surrender to it? And where is the true center? This physical Circle is a simple aid that bestows the experience of centeredness, a kind of tangible kinesthetic sense of place from the visible Circle around you, to landmarks, to the horizon, to the earth, to the solar system, to the universe. The physical Circle reminds you of who you are and it takes you into the spacious Circle of the horizon and beyond.

The center of the Circle is Peace. You *are* this peace that the unpeaceful can move within. When you remember to anchor yourself as the quiet center with a simple sigh of breath, you become the Circle as an act of self-compassion. When you forget this, the movements of thought, emotion, and body steal your peace. So, the place to begin is to be the spacious love, the open sky, to these movements.

I use the Circle as a tool, as an *idea* to lead you into an experience: the experience of your presence as an openhearted awareness that is *through* you and all *around* you. Once in the experience you must let go of the *idea* and *be* the Circle of your true presence. There is no interpreter, and there is no one to intercede on your behalf. It's a path to yourself that uses one of the oldest symbols for God - the circle - a circle with a dot in the center. A dot within a circle is called a *circumpunct*. It has been used as a symbol for many things, including the sun, and the solar system. It is both an ancient symbol for God and for the *true self.* When I invoke the Circle and ask you *to be the Circle* to everything that moves within you, I am asking you to be the all-creator of the solar system of your world and beyond where creation begins. The dot in the circle can be anything in this life, which moves within this great mystery of God. But the circled dot is your big **I** when you live at the center of the Circle

The Circle Lives Within Us

of who you are.

Symbols, words, ideas, and concepts are to enlist the aid of the mind. You must believe that this quiet center is you, this presence that is the closest thing to truth, this experience of quietly *being here.* Once you believe it, then it is about giving up *time* to it. This has a double meaning. You must spend some of your daily *clock* time *in* and *as* the Circle of *you.* But the journey to the *truth* of you, of me, of everyone, is something beyond all your history, something timeless. This Circle as a physical place and a symbol of the Self, is a tangible entrance into honoring the power of your own Oneness.

I want you to find some place special, not too far from where you live, and build your own Circle. Let your own truth come through you as to how to do it. Let the Circle tell you. From the moment you outline the Circle on the ground it begins. This Circle is a living form of your own spacious, big heartedness to all that moves within you. When you create this Circle you must divine the right spot where the sacredness and sense of alignment is already alive. Trust what you are drawn to. There are no rules, only your own sense of sacredness and truth. Let the *place* tell you what to do. Any natural thing can be part of the presence of the Circle ~ trees, rocks, and plants. The true directions are within you, not without, so anchor the directions into the place itself, into the landmarks that surround you. In the end even this Circle will do away with itself and *you* will have gone beyond it being useful to you. It may simply remain as a place sacred and special to you. It may be that you have so completely realized its truth within you that you are always sitting in the Quiet One the Circle has helped take you *to.*

No matter where you live, whether in the heart of New York City or in a mid-sized town in the Midwest, find a place where you can sit quietly with the earth. It doesn't matter if it's in your backyard or a city park, but find a tree, a rock, or a spot that you like, that is your power spot, so to speak. Don't *make* it impossible because you *believe* it's just not there. Every time we walk into a room or a place there is some spot that feels the most comfortable to us. Trust the *dowsing stick* of your body to find it for you. It's good if you can have privacy, but if you can't, let that be part of what you must be the spacious Circle *to*. You may not be able to spend time there everyday, so find a way to create a sacred Circle in your home. Even if it can only stay in place temporarily, do it. Buy a round rug that you can roll up if need be. Let these places be where you go to be *the quiet Circle that you are.* There is no failure or success here. Just do the best you can, even if that is simply the physical movement of going there and being there. If your own self-judgment is the dominant movement of the day, be the Circle to it. Be the Circle to it and practice giving up believing in your thinking.

There are many movements in this Circle, movements of the mind, movements of the emotions, movements of the body and spirit. But never forget that you *are* what they move *in*. I want you to bring into the Circle every movement that has ever moved in your soul, every life you feel you have lived, every story that was lived with only one outcome, every one of your multiple personalities, every fear, every hope, every person that has ever hurt you, loved you, hated you, helped you. But remember, this is about your soul and honoring movements that were lost and rejected. Always remember you are the bighearted Circle, which bestows the honoring, spacious, big-hearted love. It's a breath of life that gifts frozen moments with a warm compassion that allows life to live and move. You are not forgiving anyone with an idea or a thought. You are honoring your own unhonored pain, as the spacious Circle of self-love. In this way you become *forgiveness.* You are the vast, spacious loving mystery that all these separate selves move *in*. The only way you will have peace and oneness is by practicing being this everyday as much as you can. You must walk it. And in walking it you demonstrate it, and you teach it. It is important you know in your bones what this *action of true self-love* is. This is the Circle and the *Circle lives within us.*

Chapter Three

The Spine of Your Life
*The spine of our life is a form within the great Flow
where everything is connected in the web of life.
Everything we do rhythms through this web
like a sacred song.*

I once thought I knew who I was and what I wanted to do. My first true *knowing* of my work here on earth, a destined purpose, was *I'm going to be a writer*. And I wrote many things in different forms that have since become shredded paper for a rat's nest, or glued together by a leaking roof in my outdoor storage shed. I wrote from my core because writing was intimately connected with my spiritual growth. As a young man this meant it wasn't necessarily for the public. But when you write ... you *do* write for someone besides yourself ... you are linking up with some undefined *other* in the silent language of inspired thought. I wrote to explore experience on this earth and to discover the truth of myself and others. This intent was like grabbing a hold of a thread that would weave through all my life experiences; like the thread of a necklace bringing seemingly unrelated experiences together.

But imagination draws upon experience, so traveling alongside this thrust was my *wild one* equally willing to explore the unknown in a much more dangerous way. This meant pushing the edge of limitations and when you push the edge too many times it's bound to break now and then. It started breaking for me as an 11 year old boy dashing across the street with a load of newspapers to deliver and running smack into the side of a car traveling at 40 miles an hour. Over the next 15 years there were a growing collection of motorcycle and automobile accidents.

Hidden injuries to my spine, neck, and head accumulated in a mysterious way. The kind of mental focus necessary for writing diligently became impossible as I grew older. I kept at it for a while, as if swimming upstream trying to catch my thoughts that were like fish darting out of my grasp. Eventually, I surrendered and lived in the flow instead of fighting my way against it. But the reason why I would write never faded. Although I was not able to sustain enough concentration over an extended period of time required for a full-length *book*, my creative mind was able to give expression through songs. These songs reflected the work I did with people. They were written to inspire courage and a belief in themselves that they were important and had a contribution to make in this world.

In this moment, as I speak to you, I sit in the quiet of a sacred Circle on the edge of a bone white mesa. I can see the desert agave plants standing straight and tall around me. They rest on the ground like giant, thick petaled flowers, three feet in diameter. Sleeping within their core is a fifteen-foot tall, four-inch diameter stalk, waiting to burgeon once in its 30-year life span. When the moment comes one spring upon reaching their upward limit, buds burst from the tops of the stalks like praying hands opening to the sky and those buds then flare open with the brilliant colors of red and yellow. When the stalks have dried, each plant offers itself as a perfect walking stick, or the thicker base can be hollowed to birth the deep aboriginal tones of the didgeridoo. What a beautiful gift is this *thrusting spine* of the agave plant ... as an aid when we walk and as a musical instrument giving song to the desert.

As I sit here in this desert land many years later I hold the same thread in my hand as that young man, living out my own deeper spine-like thrust of why I am here ~ to discover the truth of myself and others and to share what I have learned. From the necklace of life's experiences brought together into a circle by that thread, Medicine of One dangles over my heart.

My life, your life, everyone's life is a story and within that story are little stories. The story begins with our birth.

The Spine of Your Life

But is that really where *we* begin? Where *you* begin? Is this *you* just a linear line leading from birth to death? Are *you* your *stories*? Is there a greater *you*? Is there something that transcends these stories? These are questions on the path of *who am I.* If you are reading this book then the question of *who am I* and *why am I here* are probably sitting inside of you growing stronger and stronger.

We come into this world as something impossible to duplicate. You might duplicate the physical form through genetics, but what sings through you as your gift to the world is like no other person who has walked upon the planet. We come into life to express our uniqueness as effortlessly as a tree, whose seeds *sprout* tiny *spine-like* bursts of life that reach to the open sky as energy fulfilling its purpose. It awakens and begins to express itself with a touch of water, earth, air, and sun. As it grows, the limbs are anchored into the trunk of this tree. In that anchoring, all the way down into the ground to the roots, there is an upward motion reaching for the sky. The trunk is like the *spine* of the tree, both physically and energetically.

The trunk of the tree is within the seed, just as our own uniqueness is within us right from the beginning, like a song, like a musical score that is our vibrant presence on the earth. The true self of all of us is the *same ground of being.* Imagine this ground as the ocean and we are like a drop of water emerging from it. That drop is *I Am* and its essence is *To Be.* But in the emergence from the *beingness* of that ocean something unique begins to take form.

The life force comes through that form and expressively thrusts itself into the world like the trunk of a tree. The potential of a unique human being is born. This thrust lies waiting to be freed and to sing with the essence of your gift to the world. Because it has a driving force and because your whole life is intended to align with it, I call it the ***spine of your life.***

Trees gift us with wood from which flutes can be created. Each flute has its own unique presence and energy which flows as an *unobstructed resonant sound ... its music.* This music springs from many things, the kind of wood the flute is made of, its width, length, and perhaps most importantly, the creator of the flute. Think of the maker of that flute as a *creative force* that infuses the flute with form and a soul. The song of that soul, as an unobstructed resonant sound, manifests and can be seen in the trembling of water in a glass and felt and heard as vibration in the air. The flute's resonant vibration is more than what is seen, heard, or sensed with the body. Imagine if each flute was created with a specific song as its gift to the world, with a singular force that could affect the listener. With this gift, the flute could inspire joy, invoke the feeling of peace, empower others to action, or create harmony just by *being* itself. This simple *beingness* is just part of what the flute is by nature that vibrates forth through its physical structure as a special song and has a singular resonance. This song and unique resonance is the flute's thrust in the world ~ the spine of its life.

Your presence is as unique as a handmade flute. When you live in balance and harmony your *beingness* manifests a resonant presence impossible to duplicate. It's a radiance meant to permeate every aspect of your life: work, family, social, and private time. It comes through you effortlessly when you are able to be fully present without any self-imposed obstructions. The music of you sings into the world through the spine of your life as a force that radiates out from the center of the Circle of you.

The spine of the tree continues its reach for the sky no matter what. But unlike trees and flutes, as humans we can live our lives in a way that obstructs our true vibratory presence from gifting the world. This happens throughout our lives when we function from survival, control, fear, and desire, habitually denying, condemning, and imprisoning what we feel ~ our emotions. This imprisons our music in an old story that still owns us and owns the song of our soul. Our music becomes out of harmony and is unable to sing through us and energize the spine of our life. Sound is movement, and we have prevented the life within us from moving in our efforts to survive.

Things happen to all of us just as injury and trauma can happen to trees, but trees don't have minds with thoughts that undermine the truth inherent in their seed. Trees don't think and they don't adopt beliefs that block their thrust toward the sky. We, however, in our struggle to survive can become our own greatest obstacle to the truth of *the spine of our life* thrusting forth into the world. We can convince ourselves with all of our thinking there is no sky and there is no *me*; we then believe there are only pain, sorrow, and struggle. Our stories lived in one way keep skipping back into the old groove of that *one way* detouring us away from this basic thrust of why we are here.

Our character is often shaped and driven by our stories. Much of our character is formed by how we meet experience. Inevitably for most of us we are driven by survival and getting what we want. This is a thrust and a force just like the spine of your life. But it serves the little **i** that is anchored in our stories; rather than the big **I** that transcends our stories and serves the greater you that inevitably serves the greater whole of the world.

We all want to be loved ... all of us. We all want to be happy. Somewhere along the line we begin to believe if we can get what we want we will have this happiness. But our deepest want of peace gets lost in the struggle. We struggle to get what we want from others. In pursuit of our little **i**'s *wants,* we thwart the greater purpose of our being here in the world. It can seem this greater purpose has been derailed by what happens to us, but it's really by how we engage what happens to us and our relationship to our emotional being. When we are stuck in an old story, we are aligning with the little **i**'s *spine* of our character. We separate from the thrust of our *true spine of this life.*

Even when life presents us with great challenges of survival we can still align with that true spine. I have seen people overcome seemingly insurmountable forces, obstacles, and trauma without becoming hard, cruel, indifferent, protective, or closed as they found a way to let life express itself compassionately through their unique gift to the world. These are people who found freedom through compassion beginning with *self-compassion.* Self-compassion is the great action the path of the Medicine of One invokes so you don't live life from your *story* and from the wanting that can become harmful and greedy, creating separation from others and from the truth of your being here on this earth.

You do not have to have a job in which it's clear you are benefitting all of humanity. You do not have to be a Gandhi, or a Nelson Mandela, or a Martin Luther King. It doesn't matter what your job is, a bank teller, a gas station attendant, a store clerk, a librarian, a wife, or a father. No matter what you do in life this spine is still there seeking expression and in its unobstructed form it is your gift to the world.

We are all like medicinal plants whose gifts can be a unique scent, a special form, or the ability to heal ailments in the human/animal kingdom. You can attribute this healing effect to a particular substance and try to manufacture it, but it will lack the true power of the plant, which is the *spine of its life*. Mormon Tea has bright green flexible stick-like leaves that grow straight up to the sky. In appearance it is a unique bushy plant. Visually what it gives to the world in its presence is different than any other plant. The Lemon Verbena has small sage colored leaves and can grow right next to Mormon Tea. It can often be mistaken for a weed. In their color and form they are expressively different. The Mormon Tea spine of life brings healing to the lungs. It is often used to raise blood pressure in hospitals when people are having surgery performed. Lemon Verbena has a wonderful sage-like smell with a touch of lemon. When rain is followed by the heat of a strong desert sun, the air is gifted with the beauty of its relaxing, peaceful sage scent. As a healer it can relieve digestive spasms, strengthen the nervous system, and reduce stress.

These plants effortlessly gift the world with their unique healing presence that calms and beautifies. In their simple *beingness* they can only live at the center of the Circle where the spine of their life manifests through them. They are not trying to *do* anything.

The spine of our life is no different. When we live at the center of the Circle of who we are, our *beingness* manifests a uniqueness. It comes through us effortlessly when we simply be *here*. I call this our *hereness*. From this *hereness* our music sings into the world as a force that radiates out from the center

The Spine of Your Life

of the Circle of you. In this way we become the demonstration of our spine.

Our *greater spine* is the great undercurrent of our *being here* in the *play of the world*. This undercurrent will show itself through what we naturally like and love, the unique expression of our *being here* as it expresses itself through our humanity. It is our *doingness* in life that spontaneously bursts into the world from our beingness like the flower-like being of the agave whose stalk thrusts into the world. *The flower of our being births the flower of our doing.* It is our activity, our work and our creative expression. There is no force. There is no domination. There is no control. The *spine of our life* is not tied to survival or **i**-dentity. It is anchored in the *tree trunk* of humanity and the earth, and *compassion* in all of its wonderful forms is a part of its natural expression for everyone.

This spine of our life is born from something we *are*, not something we *do*. We are this first for *ourselves* in our own life, and then it naturally radiates out into the world and others as our unique effortless gift. It is a form within the great flow where everything is connected in the web of life. Everything we do *rhythms* through this web like a sacred song.

We can get lost along the way of our journey through life, but this thrust lies within us, waiting, just like the agave stalk. The Medicine of One is a journey of cultivating your true presence by lovingly clearing away the obstacles so the spine of your life can sing forth into the world. From *true being* comes *true doing*.

Medicine of One

Chapter Four

Clear the Way
*When you clear the way,
you invoke the power of your soul.*

Walk with me in the desert. Feel the warm touch of the wind, the heat of the sun, and the smell of earth and plants. Let the wonder of your senses bring you into this moment. Your very soul is a vast library of sensorial experience and so in this moment be soulfully present as you touch with your eyes, see with your ears, listen with your body, and are awakened as you inhale the desert scents.

See the raven just above us, hovering in one place with wings spread, gently rocking to and fro, movement within the unmoving, neither going up nor down, forward nor backward and yet in constant subtle motion to maintain stillness. In this marriage of movement and stillness, hovering motionless in the gusty wind is the demonstration of meeting experience fully aware, fully engaged, fully here as a unity of will, awareness, trust, and courage ... a soul moving through experience, one with the wind, one with the sky, one with the flow. The immediate world for that raven is the ever-changing wind. If the wind comes from another direction the raven must adjust, sensing with primordial attention and then performing an action, large or small, to remain hovering in one place. The particular form of the raven's outstretched wings as a thrust of will reflects its willfulness. Now, this sensing awareness/attention and the willful, all swim in the wind as the action of trust. This trust is seen as the dance on the wind, riding the wind, give and take with the wind, yet miraculously staying in one place. They all come together as soul inhabits the raven's body and hovers in the wind. These three things come together in the moment and in the moment they are *One*.

The raven does not know what the wind is going to do before the moment in which it happens, and yet, perhaps, it senses beyond the visible something as subtle as air pressure or temperature. There is something happening in that moment that it knows will lead to the next and the raven adjusts to **ride the flow**. As a soul, its full presence comes together in awareness, will, and trust. And in that presence it is inextricably connected to the web of life and inseparable from all things. It is what it is ~ the soul of a raven dancing through life. Soul ~ what a wonderful word of magic and power. But what a mystery it is!

What is *soul?* And what is *a* soul?

Think of the soul as something unique, enlivened with life force, shaped by experience, but as subtle as the experience of color, scent, or a presence invoked by its form. The soul is not something you can hold in your hand and touch. Soulfulness is inseparable from your *hereness* in this body. We separate spirit, soul, body, and mind to talk about them. But they are meant to be unified in you're *hereness on the earth*. If the Circle is a oneness that ripples on into infinity, the soul is an experiential energy that ripples inseparably out into the greater Circle of you. The soul comes from *One Light* into this world and manifests as a *soul rainbow*. The soul is like a unique prism carved from experience through which the One Light passes. When you turn your attention upon itself you sit in the prism as that one light, as a dot within the Circle, a sun within the greater sun.

Off in the distance are two sandstone buttes, shaped by the forces of wind, water, trees, and the plants rooting in them. The trees growing in the rock chip and carve away at it through the force of their roots, which wedge and break the rock apart. So the life that grows on the butte shapes it as it supports that life. One butte is flowing and rounded like a woman lying on her back. The other is the head of a warrior gazing sternly up into the sky. The form invokes presence, a

Clear the Way

soul. The experience of that soul is the very ancient history of its life in the elements. This outer form comes into shape from the relationship between the inner form of the soul and the elemental forces of experience.

When you think of history, your personal history, your *experience,* think soul experience, *all* of your soul's experience, which is unlikely to find full expression in your present historical memory. We come here with *experience.* How that happens isn't as important as the feeling that it is true. I don't need to cultivate a belief in past lives to honor the history that seems to come from the Dreamtime. If the story resonates within me then it has a *reality* for me. How we met the experience of old stories shapes us, just like the soulful inner form and the forces of life have shaped the butte. The unlived outcomes of stories may yet lie trapped in the very atomic anatomy of the body. If we are, in fact, the whole world, then every story is within us. Partially lived stories can haunt and imprison us.

How we meet new experiences, how we adapt to them, is determined by how we met the experiences of the past. Does the experience flow through us uninhibited? Or do we reject components of the experience based upon our survival and keep the old stories cycling into the present? The choices for survival accumulate as stories lived in *one way.*

The rejection of experience and emotions coupled with rigid defensive thoughts and beliefs make the body of this life, our sacred home in this form, difficult to occupy. Rejected experience creates separation, steals our peace, and energizes our reactions to life. We cannot be soulfully present and the spine of our life cannot easily gift the world. It becomes impossible to *be here now.* Rather than unity and harmony we are out of harmony and separated. The problem is that the soul cannot fully find its home in the body of this life. The way is blocked and it cannot attend to this *NOW.*

The difference between the raven and us is that we have the ability to direct our attention back into this *presence* and know this awareness that leads us to the truth of who we are. The raven is just *being* it. However, this gift of knowing, when turned outward, becomes the dilemma and curse of human beings ~ thinking and the need to control.

One of my wolf-dog helpers was named Hanta Yo. Hanta Yo means, *clear the way*. He quickly earned his name by his action to go straight for what he wanted. He lived from a place of freedom. His soul knew no other way. He was always true to himself. His soul aligned with his true nature. He knew what he wanted. Hanta Yo's *clearing the way* had its softer side as well. He had the softest hair of any dog I have ever touched. In his service to the many people who visited us for help, he seemed to align himself with its full meaning in the Medicine of One. He gifted many people with his soft, loving presence. Some have actually told me it was this touch that freed them from the need to seek love and rooted them in the knowing that they were loved. He had a polar bear-like presence that gave them courage and brought them into the awareness of their own courage. With his unconditional love and courage, he reminded them who they are and reflected back to them their own self-compassion.

We need soul to be here now. Many people live from the heart up and many from the head up. Frozen pain occupies the space below, which prevents one from being present in this world. To clear the way is to melt down through the frozen pain with the very warmth of self-love. It is the heartfelt reentering into the unlived and the unloved experiences within ourselves, a conscious flight into the dark forgotten rejected pain as a compassionate liberating light. We reclaim our *Soulfulness* so we may live the dream of the soul in this life and reside in the reality from which it is born ~ a soul infused and dwelling in the Great Spirit, the oneness of the Circle of godliness that we are. This is the new choice, the path to what you want.

Clearing the way is like breaking a part of yourself out of prison with compassion. It's an act of liberation. To be free is to be free of all history, all stories. Experience is a dance that invokes the mind, emotion, and body. The soul is the dancer. This freedom and liberation is a return of the rhythm, flexibility, and strength of the *limbs of the soul*.

The raven trusts the wind and surrenders to it. It takes courage to move forward, out of the controlling that

Clear the Way

knows, into the unknown. The need to control is driven by the fear of death ~ the fear of the death of this dream called *you, me,* i. It takes courage to die. It's a step out of a life of survival toward the center of the Circle of truth. Through self-loving, the *reality of fear* is dissolved, your music is freed and sings through the spine of your life. You can more easily reside in the home of who you are. The soul, fully rooted in the *home of now,* is capable of living free from history as it stands in the arms of the Great Spirit. The Medicine of One is *being a love* that *clears the way.* Strangely enough it takes courage to love your*self* as you give up the safety of your thinking mind and anchor your head in your heart. *Awareness, will, and trust are unified to bring you to the center of the Circle of who you are.*

Your body is the sacred home of the soul in this life born from the One from which we often use the word God, Great Spirit. The name isn't important. When I ask you to take my hand as I support you as the Circle, I am demonstrating this greater Circle of you taking your hand and leading you courageously forward. Awareness, will, and trust come together into this world courageously as self-compassion, a world as unpredictable as the raven's world of the wind.

We walk together. And as we walk through the garden of ourselves and encounter impasses, the way is cleared. Through the invocation of this compassionate *One* that you are, a radiant presence of truth as tangible as the greater you wrapping its arms around your very soul's pain, we *clear the way.* We walk with it and we free it as we invoke it. From the first moment of letting something move inside of you, without impeding it, you are learning the Medicine of One.

Until you have walked the Circle of this book, much of the meaning of what I say will remain a question and mystery. Don't worry about that. Understanding comes from the walk. Spread the wings of your suffering to the open sky of your own compassion and fly back *home to the now in your body.* That moment can begin right now.

Medicine of One

Chapter Five

Thinking

*If you can understand, give up believing
in your thinking and give up being right
... that's it. That's you as the Circle.*

What is thought? Who is thinking? Who is talking? And who are we listening *to*? And *believing*? Where is the answer to the question "Who am I" in all of this confusion? The answer lies in the one who is listening, not the one who is talking. So right here, plain and simple, is the error. We think and we believe what we think and because thinking can be so constant and dominant in our life our experience of *who we are* is wrongly established in this thinking.

When you establish *who you are* in the action of thinking, your experience is a world of many voices: the voice of the warrior who defends by attacking with hard confidence and tough courage, the voice of the victim who fears, worries, and doubts, and the voice of shame, guilt, and self-blame that undermines true worth. These voices are many and when you root yourself in them you live in a world of confusion and separation. These are the spins in the Circle of who you really are. In their spinning they think endlessly. This is what I mean by the little **i** with the spinning dot that is a head. These many voices invoke points of view with thoughts, which can be diametrically opposed to one another. They think profusely because they live from survival. The majority of thinking is driven by the exercise of control, controlling the world around us and the world within us. The world within is an emotional world we are trying to suppress because survival means rejecting the fragile, the powerless, the helpless, the valueless, and the unsafe, which cannot defend themselves. The emotional energies, which are rejected, are the fuel that continually energizes all the thinking.

Thought is movement and thoughts carry a force. You can be at their mercy or be greater than them. The thinking I am talking about is the thinking involved in controlling our experience that moves us further away from the center and our truth. This thinking keeps things emotionally distant from us, since the point of our doing it is to distance ourselves from unwanted feelings. It creates tension, restricts breathing, and separates us from the *awareness of deep listening*, a very different use of the mind.

Thinking. What happens when there is something, a person, a situation, a discussion in your head and you can't stop thinking about it? It can go on for days or more and you can't stop the endless flow of thoughts. Why? What is all the thinking attempting to accomplish? If there is anything your mind keeps returning to it means there is fear there somewhere. All of the thinking is trying to resolve that which is threatening your value, your power, your safety through the effort to understand and control so you can feel better. If the tense thoughts have something to do with someone else, then you are undoubtedly trying to arrive at a result where *you are right*. This is the more mundane, everyday, obsessive thinking.

The key word is *threat*. What you are threatened by will depend on your unintegrated history and the unmoved emotional charges that get set into motion again and again, generating thinking to control and resolve the disturbance upsetting you to allow you to feel that you are *right*. Or, maybe you have behaved in a way you are judging as *wrong* so your thinking is full of self-judgment, even shame. There may be a reality to this, and there may not be, based on your history of experience. Much thinking goes on in the imagination and the scenarios we imagine stimulate more thinking. Thoughts feed on themselves energizing more thinking. And you have the opposites, *right* and *wrong,* creating movement. If you hang on to *right* then you invoke its opposite, *wrong*.

The world of thinking is set in motion when you are

Thinking

born. First there is the little *i*, you as an infant, who has emerged out of the absolute ocean of being, the mother's womb, been given a name, and you begin to *want.* Once you begin to walk and learn the language of thought, that dot on the *i* begins to spin. But you are still able to be in the big **I** at times, in the child's world of magic and the oneness of life until you are taught that living in that world is not normal and your *original truth* is abandoned from the need of *wanting to be loved.* This begins about the time you are learning the language of your parents, which is the language of thought. Over time thinking becomes your *i-dentity.* Unless you wake up from the world of thinking, this false identity can persist until the day you die.

Thinking. We journey so far away from the center of the labyrinth of our true self, that we don't know the feeling of true presence and self. Our Circles become hijacked by our *protector controller* ... the dominant personality force of our survival. If you are reading this book, you realize there must be something more to *you*, *me* and *us* than thinking.So now you begin your walk back to the center in this labyrinth of the self. It seems like you are learning, or relearning, but you are really just clearing the way by liberating unmoved emotion which drives thinking. That little *i* with the spinning dot of thinking has a library of spins it has tried to control and throw out of the Circle. The action of bringing into the Circle rejected experience frees the trapped energy that creates your worldview and generates the assumptions and reactions that push you into thinking. The trapped emotional energy is both the fuel for all the thinking and the creator of the lens that determines how you view the world. It's like a mouse driving a wheel as it chases after its own shadow. What you see is determined by beliefs that hold trapped emotions in place, and the energy of those trapped emotions keeps you spinning. The only way to stop the vicious cycle is to stop believing in your thinking.

Our first step is awareness. If you walk with bare feet through an area of broken glass, you must be aware. In this moment you are not thinking. You are just present and aware in the moment. When you walk across a creek on stones jutting up, this awareness allows an *instinctive knowing* to carry you across the creek ~ unless your fear *owns* you ... and you think. Then you fall. This reinforces the *belief* that you need to think and think more because you don't want to fall again. Thinking creates the problem and then more thinking tries to solve the problem and it goes on and on.

But what if you choose to stop believing your thinking and getting involved with it? What if you chose to break the cycle by just being present, and *here?* With this new choice, as you take that first step, you are aware that you have stopped breathing and your body is tensing. You are standing up straight and stiff and the unvoiced thought of falling is starting to own you. Before one fearful thought leads to the next you breathe and relax, sink down through your knees and feet, and stop thinking ... and all goes well.

This is the same progression that happens when you push an emotional movement out of the Circle because it threatens your feeling of being in control. You stop breathing, your body tenses up, and the fear, which you have tensed around, drives your thinking, and thinking fuels your fear and creates more thinking. To remain established in your thinking is to cut yourself off from the awareness that will lead you back to the center of the truth of who you are. Note that I haven't used the phrase *established in your mind* because thinking and analytical thought is only one aspect or action of the mind. Prior to the movement of thought is presence and awareness. When this awareness is turned back on itself, it is the true self. Awareness is the unmoving mind. It is still and quiet. It is the Quiet One.

There is a listener in the midst of all this thinking and these many *voices.* Your awareness is this listener. This awareness is at first cultivated as a kind of witness or observer. But it must not be an observer that separates and disassociates from the emotional movements. It is with an awareness that engages, penetrates, embraces, and touches these movements as *the true action of self-love, as the compassionate Circle of you.* This is your presence and awareness that is prior to thought. This presence is all-encompassing. It is the Circle that everything moves in. You are keenly aware, but your attention is allowed to sink back into itself. This is the, *abide in the aware-*

Thinking

ness, which leads to the full presence of the *quiet that you are.* It was always there, sitting quietly amidst all the noise ... *listening.*

Thinking is the *great obstacle to peace.* Whatever it is you *can't stop thinking about,* bring it closer into the Circle. Bring it up close, right in front of you. Whatever the object you are thinking about, gift it the godly presence of your breath and allow every ripple of emotion to move. This object is some person, situation, something that your thinking is swirling around. If you are under foreclosure and losing your house, bring the house, the people you might be disputing with, the mortgage company, or anything else your thinking and emotions are swirling around into the Circle with your imagination. You do this to bring your emotions closer to you, rather than to distance yourself through thinking. Bring your every fear and worry into the Circle. Bring in people and things you fear and worry about, especially the ones your thoughts have been dancing around

Don't talk to it, don't think about it, be present with it, with every possible feeling and emotion it can arouse in you. If you find you can't stop thinking ... then feel ... get closer to the energy driving the thinking ... and just *Be the Circle* to it. Breathe ... relax ... let all the feelings go everywhere through you and around you. It will get quiet ... and the quiet might make you restless ... and the mind will find another object to grapple with. Bring it close up again ... and again ... and again. This is turning the mind to face itself. When this happens, the only thing that is there is your awareness. There is no thinker ... only thinking.

The mind wants to move and wants to attend to some *thing*, an object it can engage. When the mind faces itself, what you are doing is directing the mind's attention into itself. They melt into one another and in this melting you establish yourself as the compassionate Circle that allows movement. This is simply allowing your thinking to be just another movement in the Circle. Thoughts are energy. Emotions are energy. Your body is energy. Your very soul is energy. You as the Circle are the *Sun full of all this energy.* But you are the whole, not all the separate movements. Believing and getting involved in your thinking separates you from this whole.

Thinking, thoughts, and beliefs are all the same. A belief is a thought, an idea, which is *believed to be true.* So thinking does not have to always be experienced as a conversation in your head. Your worldview is a host of beliefs that are thoughts, which determine your reactions and behavior in the world.

Because the feelings of powerlessness and helplessness are at the core, often when I am trying to lead someone into these feelings, a posture and energy will enter them to block the way. This posture holds the thought that these weak and fragile feelings are unacceptable. But at the moment, the mind isn't actively thinking this is unacceptable. The thought is there in the background energizing their posture. These hosts of thoughts we have about the world are forces that invoke postures of defense and protection. So there are thinking, thoughts, and then beliefs. It's important to know what you believe. Emotions can move through you, but if you hold on to a belief about a story in your life the same emotions keep recycling through you.

Believe that you are this Circle of compassion so you can be who you are. When the feeling of compassionate presence is firmly there, you don't need to work at holding onto to it. Have faith in it.

If you can understand *give up believing in your thinking and give up being right,* have great faith you are a compassionate presence, and let life move through you ~ that's you as *the Circle*. From this faith just walk the path and be free.

Chapter Six

Loss of Deep Listening

*Deep listening occurs when the experience and
the experiencer are One. There is no separation.
There is no subject and object.
You are in the flow on the river of life.*

When I rode my motorcycle through the Black Mountains and over the top of *Blue Mountain Flat On Top* on a winding up and down road, through the rhyolite rock, through the gateway to the Verde Valley, I was listening keenly to the road with all my attention. With my foot pedals igniting sparks every now and then as they kissed the pavement, my eyes were in deep listening far ahead guiding me to adjust to a patch of gravel or oil, a car slowed to a snail's pace around a bend up ahead, or a coyote, squirrel, rabbit, or deer running across the road. The body and the bike were one as we leaned into the curves as if rocked in the cradle of the road. The rush of wind past my ears sang a changing song according to my speed and angle to the road. I was abiding in complete awareness. There was no me, no road, no bike, no cliffs, no sky, no wind. It was the flow of One ignited with adrenaline ~ it was **deep listening**. But was there peace and compassion? I will leave that for you to answer.

If we could take the alertness we have in activities and sports that require our complete attention, remove the adrenaline, and sit in an unmoving state this would be true deep listening. This is one of the reasons people become addicted to extreme and dangerous sports. It's the only time they can enter the flow and experience supreme deep listening. But it takes the danger and threat that fuels them with a rush to deliver them into the moment where they are infused with absolute awareness. They must abide in this awareness or die. If you could hold this kind of commitment without the adrenaline - in complete stillness - this commitment that *I must abide in this awareness or die,* you would have absolutely nothing to worry about because there would be no thinking mind to worry.

When that raven I spoke of in *Clear the Way* rides the wind, it's in a state of deep listening; eyes, wings, tail ... all listening as that unity of awareness, will, and trust. This is the listening, which is your *beingness.* It flows from the quiet that you are. When you are having a conversation with someone, it might seem you can't talk and listen at the same time, but you can. The listening I am talking about isn't associated with sound. It's a way to describe profound attentiveness. You are attending to a deeper flow. This listening allows you to ride the surf to the center of the labyrinth. Without it you will lose your balance and be sucked into the spinning undertow of the mind.

Because our minds are so allied to our survival and because we are struggling to survive from the first breath of air we take, our trust becomes misplaced. Instead of surrendering to the greater Oneness we are born from, this mental controlling survivalist force rules our Circle. Because this controlling force functions primarily from fear, we can't hear the deeper truth because we don't know how to trust.

This listening becomes the active walking of the path to the truth of who you are. It is this *listening* that brings you the experience which answers the question *Who am I?* I say *path* because it is like learning to walk. You don't learn to walk by waiting for your legs to move. You begin on your stomach, then you get up on your knees, you crawl and then at some point an amazing thing happens. For the first time you stand on your own two feet, maybe with help, and then you do it without any help. There is a little help with those first few steps and finally the magic moment when something inside you *knows* walking. You walk and you never forget. And just

Loss of Deep Listening

maybe this walking is a remembering of something you already knew.

Translate this into levels of *listening*. Feel yourself in these moments of transition as you move out of a natural deep listening presence. First, in the womb, something enters the human fetus as a unique presence ... unique, but inseparable even as it bathes in amniotic fluid like a drop in the ocean that's still inseparable from that ocean. Feel yourself as this thoughtless presence that is still so close to what is not born and what does not die. Now feel your birth and the birth of awareness as the dot in the Circle begins. *You* begin and awareness begins. *Your world* begins, and you begin your journey of survival. In this beginning *you are the deep listening.* But part of your survival will be a disconnection that results in not listening, not knowing, not feeling. Abandoning your emotional world will be part of how you survive. What was once natural becomes *unnaturally unlearned.* But your true self's first manifestation as I is this deep listening presence that evolves into awareness, which leads to awareness of the world ... which leads to the experience of separateness.

The big I is separated into the little i. That moment when you get up off the floor and walk is also when you take a definitive step into this little i and begin to separate from the big I. The next step will be when that little *you* begins talking. Talking and walking - ah! The praise, the attention - *Give me more! I think I will giggle and laugh and do a little dance.* Now you learn that how you behave determines the quality of attention you receive.

We want loving, appreciative attention. So you mold yourself to that at the expense of what you are really feeling. You begin to learn how to put on a *smiling mask,* which seems to allow you to control how others respond to you. You separate from your true presence and unlearn the deep listening, which is just being in intimate contact with the truth of you and how you feel in the moment where the big I is. You are losing the deep listening that connects you with the One ... and everyone around you encourages you to do so. You have entered the maze that will create confusion until you choose to awaken your listening and journey through the labyrinth of

Medicine of One

self. In this stage of your childhood the most immediate desire is *I want to be loved*. Your want is not a thought anymore than hunger is a thought. You want warmth that brings safety. We need this *Circle of love* to become emotionally healthy.

Now there is you and everyone else: you and the others who can give you what makes you feel good. You have a hunger for a particular kind of experience that depends on *others*. Now you are the experiencer who wants a particular kind of experience that is provided to you from another human, from something *other* than you. Your need and hunger cause you to split off from the flow of your deep listening. You listen as a *hungry ghost*. The experiencer and the experience are no longer unified. You have separated from your *deep listening* forsaking your journey to the true self in the labyrinth, and entered the maze of wanting with the thinking mind as your guide. Without this deep listening it will be as if you grabbed a *false thread that will lead you to a false center*. Seeking true love and peace, you reach outward toward others giving them the power to determine your centeredness.

Worry becomes the great block to trust and deep listening. Worry presents many options as well as the worry of which thread to choose. Deep listening follows one thread of truth. But the thread lies hidden beneath the louder noise of the worrying mind. Consider invoking your deeper listening that penetrates beneath the rapid motions of the thinking mind. Consider committing yourself to deep listening.

See with your ears. Listen with your eyes. Smell with your whole body. If what you hear is the *quiet*, *this* is the *listening* I am talking about. I am not talking about the voices of spirits or God speaking in the human language. This *listening* I am speaking of hears what is there before language and stalks through the woods of *Who Am I*. Its prey is the origin of thought. The mind that *listens* sees itself as hunter and prey merged into *One,* as they become the *unmoving* Circle in which they move. *This listening* is not your mind looking for tangible answers you can hold like an object in your hands, nor is it a seeing that can delineate what it has found.

Deep listening occurs when the experience and the experiencer are *One*. There is no separation. There is no subject

Loss of Deep Listening

and object. You are in the *flow* on the river of life. The *true thread* leads you to your own loving presence. The *true action of self-love* is made possible by this presence that *listens* before thought. You grasp the thread as this action of deep listening. As this listening you follow the thread of truth *home*.

Medicine of One

Chapter Seven

Nothing Gets Thrown Out of the Circle

If there is such a thing as One, how can anything be refused or denied as being part of that One?

In 1975, at the age of 25, I kissed death on the lips. On March 5 of that year I buried my father in a snowy grave in Lansing, Michigan. For the next three weeks I completely rebuilt an Austin Healy 3000 in my Uncle Norvie's garage. I went as far as buffing down the rods, putting a whole new engine block in and added a fresh paint job.

Several days after completing the Healy a friend accompanied me in a separate car, and we headed back home to the west coast, where I had a cabin near the ocean in the Santa Cruz Mountains in California. Somewhere on I-70, not too far from Richfield, Utah, I opened her up and flipped her into overdrive, racing up to 130 miles an hour. It's worth mentioning that a half an hour prior to this I took a Quaalude, a muscle relaxer, and chased it with a beer. For some reason, I glanced off to my side for a moment and ran smack into a guidepost. I overreacted by cranking the wheel to the left, flipped over, and slid 330 feet upside down. These cars were known as ragtops because the convertible top was little more than a flimsy frame with a rag of vinyl thrown over it. Later, when the car was towed to a gas station, you could see the steering wheel had been partially shaved off in the slide. My head and shoulder struck the same pavement. But in some uncanny way, I managed to dive deep into the belly of the overturned Healy, preventing me from being beheaded.

If you can understand the magnitude of this accident, then it becomes equally understandable that I could easily have died or at the very least been paralyzed from the neck down. I lay unconscious beneath the wreck for 15 or 20 minutes until my friend, who had been driving behind me, managed to flag down someone to help him flip the car over. Before they actually attempted that, I came to, heard the electric fuel pump clicking away, managed to find the key in the dash and turn the ignition to the off position. Then I heard someone calling to me. From the pitch black, I called back, "Get me outta here!"

Somehow the two of them managed to flip the car on its side. I crawled out and stood up. They both looked at me as if they were staring at the dead. The man who had helped my friend was a doctor, and he immediately fled the scene. I glanced at the car, turned to my friend and said, "Let's get out of here."

He made me stop at a local clinic, where they picked the glass out of my head and wrapped it in a white turban. The next morning my neck was as stiff as day old gum. The pavement had chewed a hole through the shoulder of a leather coat, a leather vest, and into the leather of my skin, where there is still a scar. My hair was equally scraped off from a spot on the right top of my head. My legs seemed to work okay and the pain and stiffness were tolerable. A Justice of the Peace collected two hundred dollars for reckless driving and I jumped into my friend's car and headed for California. I was like a tough cowboy, thrown off a horse, who just dusted off his jeans and got back on his horse, never thinking twice about getting myself checked or examined for injuries.

This is a perfect metaphor for how many of us deal with our pain and trauma. We walk away from it. We toughen and harden to it. And then we pay a heavy price for it, just like I have in this instance. The physical, mental, and emotional challenges this experience brought me have proven to be my greatest teacher. They have taught me *the true action of self-*

Nothing Gets Thrown Out of the Circle

love. Walking away, denying our pain, smiling habitually when we are angry or sad is the opposite of this true action. These actions are a rejection of some part of our immediate experience, which is then forgotten, and we lose some of the radiance of our living soul. In essence we are pretending to be okay through our *attempt* to throw them out of the *Circle of who we are*. Those emotions, which we refuse to acknowledge and *feel*, are like anchors tied to ropes tethered around us. We sink deeper and deeper into a kind of immobility. Safe perhaps, but close to the living-dead, we unconsciously seek whatever means we can to medicate the forgotten pain. Forgotten pain breeds fearful thinking and creates suffering. Life has pain, physical and emotional. But can we still have peace and be free of the mind's spin of suffering?

In the Medicine of One the *shadow* never seemed like an appropriate word for what has been thrown out of the Circle. It always seemed like a judgment of what we have rejected as dark. *Shadow* implies it is somehow dark in contrast to the light around it. It is rejected because it is unwanted, but calling it the shadow becomes part of the problem. In deep darkness where there is no light, there are no shadows. Shadows are created by light. A shadow is where there is less light on the ground of projection. A shadow is where an object has blocked the light. Because we take the projected image as the reality, truth or *true image,* we mistake these objects as the dark. The unwanted within us have been withheld from the light of love and thrown into the darkness, where they don't even cast a shadow. The more light that shines on an object from an angle, the more defined the shadow. Rather than shadows, these *unwanted ones* are like the whites of a child's eyes peering out at us in the dark, waiting for the light of our compassion. Seeing them as shadows becomes the dark we project upon them.

When you condemn the weak within, the victims with their tears and self-pity, you make them all homeless urchins in the dark, cast out of the *idea of who you think you are*. But in this dungeon of condemnation you have created, they become a witch's brew, which slowly drains the life out of you. Some of our own light and life gets trapped within them because they are still a part of us. They are our rejected parts, and in being rejected they cry and scream for mercy, to be heard, to be acknowledged ~ to be brought back into the Circle of your love.

Sometimes it can feel as if we have different personalities within ourselves. These *many* can be at odds with one another and create great conflict. Peace is made through honoring *what they feel,* not through believing *what they think.*

Our rage can burn in the dark, burn in our stomachs and bowels like a hot coal refusing to be extinguished. So, this idea of the dark and the shadow can escalate into a demon where we are victimized and demonized from within to the point where we actually convince ourselves and believe we have evilness within us. Rage is a powerful energy, that when trapped, hated, and denied, can indeed possess us and leave a trail of *evil* behavior.

A middle-aged man named Robert, whose whole life had been filled with rage, once came to me. He had been to numerous people for help and although he had gained some *control* over his rage, he was still not free. This angry violent feeling was directed toward others as well himself.

One of my tools to help people clear the way is *Soul Dreaming.* I dream the unwanted energies of the soul through myself and bring them into the awareness of a person to be integrated and felt. In this case the story needed a very dramatic form that could be considered an alternate life. Through our work we discovered a story of Robert, a woman, and his brother. In the story they all loved each other. The woman was Robert's true love, but she and his brother had come together romantically. In a blind rage Robert killed his brother. In that moment his rage was trapped in a prison of great guilt.

On our way to the Circle, I had picked up a large stick. In my mind, I saw Robert using it to beat something. When we arrived at the Circle I showed him what I wanted him to do. Beating the rock with *killer* rage, I yelled, "I'm sorry!" I never ask anyone to do anything that I won't do. As often happens in these moments of *demonstrating* I was seized with a new awareness of a complicated emotional energy that transcends the ability to describe. The combination of the specific action that energizes the specific words spoken, invokes an energy

Nothing Gets Thrown Out of the Circle

the mind cannot invoke by thinking. At the same time, if the person performs the movement without trying to figure out why they are doing something or what it means, the defensive forces of the mind are bypassed and there is an instantaneous shift. This happens just by invoking the energy and feeling it.

Robert was here to be freed from a lifetime of rage so he did not hesitate. He beat the rock *to death* over and over as he yelled, "I'm sorry!" When I sensed the feeling was filling him I asked him to stop, breathe, drop the stick, and completely relax his whole body. The sudden combination of these separated energies of killer rage, guilt, and pleading for forgiveness that was silently hidden within, brought him to his knees weeping. The soul dream I had done for him had initiated this movement and brought into his awareness the *dynamics of the story*. It allowed him to be in agreement with me, to trust me. He accepted it with his mind as a thought. But this acceptance needed to be taken further into *the true action of self-love*. He brought it into the Circle of his loving awareness by *invoking the energy* and relaxing around it as a compassionate breath of liberation.

He stood up from his kneeling position and gazed into the distance. I know when something has instantaneously shifted by a softening in the eyes and body, combined with a rooted strength. It was as if for the first time Robert was fully here on this earth.

"How do you feel?" I asked him.

"Lighter," he said, "And I like myself in this lightness."

He wrote to me after returning home to say he was finally free of his rage and thanked me. His guilt had never been connected to his rage and that was why it had never moved. He had projected his own jealousy onto others and reacted to it in anger. Then he would feel guilty for his behavior. It was a vicious cycle of rage and guilt.

When we cast parts of ourselves out from the small Circle of our identity, we reinforce that illusion of identity, and separate ourselves from the true Circle of who we are. This separation caused Robert to suffer.

To me the shadow is what we project onto all we judge in the world, be it other people, countries, cultures, reli-

Medicine of One

gions, or tribes. We project onto others what we have cast out within ourselves, and in our bright righteousness shining upon them, cast a shadow as a mirror of the dark within us. We have judged and condemned these outcast parts of ourselves to the darkness, believing they are that darkness.

Casting out our undesirable feelings and thoughts, suppressing what we think of as the *shadow*, often causes people to polarize and almost flee into the light. These people are often very ungrounded because these trapped energies stand between them and the earth. They cannot fully inhabit their body. They are stuck in the identity that is the little **i** of spirituality. Feelings that are judged as dark and unacceptable to *their self-image of light and love* become unmoved energies, blocking the way to their rooting in the earth. True peace and tranquility come from the union of dark and light. Darkness is not separated from light as a shadow cast on the ground.

What we desire to get rid of and attempt to throw out of our Circle is anything we pretend isn't there, any situation we walk away from to avoid the feelings it arouses in us, anything we block and don't allow to move, and any feelings we don't like in ourselves. This can include emotions initiated through trauma that are unconsciously frozen and forgotten. So rather than call these the *shadow,* let us call them the *forgotten unloved ones.* They are the spinning charges of energy in our Circle that we have been *trying* to *throw out of the Circle.* The key word here is trying; a force of rejection and resistance that energizes them. What was one *Circle of wholeness* is now separated and divided into shadow and light, good and bad, wanted and unwanted.

Draw a Circle in the dirt and feel that Circle as an aid to connect you to all things as circular movements, rippling into the infinity of One. Sit there as the choice to sit in what is unlimited and undivided, your deep peace and compassion. This is the *choice* that *nothing gets thrown out of the Circle.*

You can restrict, deny and, suppress and because of these choices you will sit in the separated Circle of the little **i**. In the world *that you have chosen*, you **can** throw the *forgotten unloved ones* out of the Circle of your **love**. This is a world where you have chosen to be the little **i**. The attempt to judge

Nothing Gets Thrown Out of the Circle

and restrict movements within you gives the Circle in the dirt the reality of a border, a wall. Now there is what you want and what you don't want.

The paradox is you can't throw them out of your true oneness. This little **i** sits in the big **I** of *One* where in truth nothing can be thrown out of the Circle. In your world of separation outside your wall of protection lay these *unloved forgotten one's.* They are sitting there waiting for the light of your awareness, which extends the Circle as compassion beyond any limit, and is the path back *Home.*

The only dark side of the soul is the one that we have turned away from. It is not a dark thing in and of itself. There is no shadow that holds these feelings captive in the *room of the shadow. We* hold them there through actions of defense, protection, and control, which breed a great chorus of thinking.

Thoughts will be born from these *spins in the Circle.* Give them loving space too ... but don't become involved and believe their thinking. We have many spins in our Circle, many personalities, each weaving their own web of thought. We get entangled in these webs, confused and uncertain of what our truth is.

Do not believe your thinking ... any of it. The truth is in the stillness of the mind, not its movement. It moves in response to something and that response is often determined by our unresolved incompletely lived history. Which means at some level it is birthed from fear. It is the fear that must be given spacious love and from that self-compassion comes freedom. The force within us, which pushes for success and perfection, is tight, not open ... and it is a great critic of the weak within and its foster child is *failure.*

The key to what we want to unlock - our hidden talents, gifts, and life force - does lie in shadow country. But the problem isn't the shadow. The problem lies in our selective gaze, where we shine the light of our awareness and what we choose not to see, and ultimately, not to feel. The Medicine of One is about aligning with the truth of who you are to clear the way to that truth ~ one undivided, unseparated *whole.* This is why nothing can be thrown out of the Circle: not our out of balance victim or warrior, not our rage or powerlessness, or

Medicine of One

our helplessness. Nothing, absolutely nothing is rejected.

Today the pain in my neck and head are quite dominant. For the most part, I am able to not give it my attention. But, when it does seem to drastically affect my nervous system and brain, the best I can do is remember that I am not my body, while my body screams an opposite chorus. These are the most difficult times to be the Circle and give space to the desperation ~ I mean the visceral angst of it all. It's as if some part of me is still trapped beneath that car. It is usually best for me to lie down and just be quiet. The more I try to force myself into activities, the more I run into my inability to do anything. We all have this pusher. The more it pushes, the more we fail, and the more the tension builds as we fall short of the idea of who we think we are. In a sense, it is an *idea* that is pushing. It is an *idea* of who we think we are supposed to be.

The first thing to remember about the Medicine of One, is that *nothing gets thrown out of the Circle* ... absolutely nothing. When you bring back into the Circle that which you have cast out, it is as if the radiant light of the Circle, which is you, has no single source of light that has an angle, so no point of view, therefore no judgment ~ no judgment that creates a shadow. The Circle is alive with the radiance of your own affectionate awareness, a liberating light. All parts of us are movements in their purity which, if simply allowed to move and breathe and complete themselves, rejoin the One from which they were born. And though these movements may invoke beliefs in thinking, believe them not, but be spacious to their dance. Only *you* have this power that is born of trust and surrender.

Part Two

ACTION

Medicine of One

To be the Circle is a journey to the truth of who you are as you clear the way to your deep listening, and enter the flow that carries you home. To be the Circle is to be who you are. How beautiful to live in the world being who you truly are.

From *The Circle of Life*
Lomakayu

Chapter Eight

The Journey
*You are here to be **HERE**.*
*The journey is the journey to this **HERE**.*

      The journey to the center is not a straight line. In their myths, the Hopi speak of the great migrations in which they journeyed in the four directions to where the land meets the sea until a cross was created ~ a cross with a center. The center was not apparent until the migrations ended, because the center was not where four lines of the directions met. It was a place of empowerment that could only be felt upon their arrival. This *place* was on the Colorado Plateau, which spreads out over 130,000 square miles into four states, Utah, Colorado, New Mexico and Arizona. It is considered by geologists to be a very stable landmass and capable of surviving many potential cataclysms predicted by both scientists and seers that could shake the whole earth. In their myths, the Hopi reference previous *ends of the known world.* The world has ended more than once and the fifth world is currently upon us. The 3rd world ended when the two twin heroes, Pöqánghoya and Palöngawhoya, switched places causing the ocean to be hurled over the continents of the earth ~ the great flood. Scientists have determined the poles have reversed as many as eleven times in the earth's history. Mammoths have been found in Siberia suddenly frozen with tropical vegetation still in their stomachs. In an instant, climates changed from tropical to artic and vice versa.

Medicine of One

When the great flood was upon them the Hopi migrated across the Pacific Ocean over seven "stepping stones," one of which was the Hawaiian Islands, and eventually landed in Central America. Here, they were instructed by their earth god, Maasaw, who is also the god of fire and death, to migrate in the four directions to where the land meets the sea and then turn around and come back. Once these movements were completed they were to settle at the center place where the lines all meet: the center of a cross. This place at the center was called *Oraibi - place where the earth is solid.* In this center, where the Hopi still live, they embrace the responsibility for keeping the world in balance as part of the spine of the whole tribe. They do this not only by living at the center place but also through their actions of ceremony, dance, music, and thought, which vibrate out into the world. This is part of the path of being a traditional Hopi.

The parallels between this tribal responsibility of living at the center and living at the center of your own personal Circle of self can clearly be seen. When you live at the center of the Circle of who you are this Circle is connected to the whole world without separation. This means by living from this center in your own immediate everyday world, a vibration ripples out into the greater world to keep it in balance and harmony. This is the best thing you can do for the whole world.

Just as the Hopi journeyed to the center of their own grand labyrinth to arrive at a *place of solid ground*, we too must journey to the center of the self ... a journey to solid ground where we vibrate through our presence as the *spine of our life* and gift the world. In this place of solid ground no matter what happens in the world outside of you, if you remain committed to the path of living there, the directions are truly within you. So when the *earth* of your world reverses and shifts, you remain with your feet on the ground. With your feet on the ground you realign with the true north of your*self*.

What does it mean to have solid ground under your feet? What does it mean to dwell in a place that can survive the greatest traumas? Being *grounded* is a very common term associated with stability and peace. What causes us to be ungrounded? The word *ungrounded* means the inability to

The Journey

occupy NOW, this moment. All our unmoved history blocks the way. The journey through the labyrinth is equally a journey through the psycho-emotional-physical terrain of your own physicality as a human being on this planet. You are *here* to be **HERE.** The journey is the journey to this **HERE.**

If you have the *feeling* of having no center, like a ship adrift on the sea without the power to move or the inner compass to direct and guide, then finding your center is the journey of *coming home to yourself.* It's a journey that listens to the ground to unite the sky and the earth.

Sometimes the journey can be very literal as it was with the Hopi, a movement from one location to another. In my own physical journey I began in southwest Michigan, then launched out to adventure in Philadelphia's Germantown. After that I headed west in a VW Beetle and arrived in California in a mere 48 hours, singing to myself to stay awake. I arrived at UC Berkeley and San Francisco, then eastward again from one coast to the other to New York City, across the ocean to the Far East of the China Sea, south to the Panama Canal, back to New York City, onward to Taos, New Mexico, and then back to the West Coast to Los Angeles. Finally, I came back to the Southwest and central Arizona. In fact, two miles from me is a little place called Centerville, which is the exact geographical center of Arizona. Having arrived at the center point, now I must walk the path that keeps me anchored here.

Places and geographical locations can mirror our inner journey. They did for me. But the journey is within, a journey that can be lived even if you stay in one physical location your whole life. The true migrations are a journey to the center of *yourself.* But even that statement is an illusion. How can you journey to something you already are and always have been? The journey is more about removing the obstacles. Your awareness *lights the way* and true compassion *clears the way* home. Some people's journeys are gypsy like, and others are more stationary. Many Native Americans were nomadic, while others were sedentary farmers. You don't need to be a farmer to *cultivate* truth. And you don't need to be a gypsy to acquire experiential wisdom. Truth and wisdom are who you are as descriptions of your compassion, adjectives to that state of being the Circle.

At some point you have to *awaken in the dream* and choose to live consciously if you want peace. Consciousness is not the thinking mind. The thinking mind is like a spider's web spinning out of consciousness. It's the labyrinth turned into a maze. A labyrinth is quite simple. It has one entrance and one route that twists and turns but carries you to the center. All you have to do is follow the route. A maze can have many entrances, branches, and dead ends. It generates confusion. The more you try to think your way out, the more lost you get. In the maze you are guided by desire, hunger, and fear, which mean control and a lot of thinking.

The real *you* is right there before the spinning begins. Will the maze *live* you, *polarize*, and *magnetize* you into the endless spin of cycles, which never lead to the center? Or will you wake up and choose to clear the way and walk the labyrinth to the center that has always been there?

The clarity of the path and clearing the way wasn't always present in my awareness. Yes, I felt my life was a path of waking up. But there were many times when I was a blind man feeling the walls inch by inch to guide me forward. And forward would sometimes mean going backward, for the walls of the maze are mirrors of the unmoved emotions in our soul's history. So in a sense we can't just bulldoze our way to the center. We have to turn around and face the frozen moments of the past to clear the way to the center and transform the maze into a labyrinth of simplicity. This is how forward becomes backward. This is why what we think we have already dealt with revisits us.

It might have appeared as if my reasons for journeying around the globe were not aligned to that center. But if you are here to live awake in the dream, once you start ... there is no turning back. You may stumble hundreds of times, but always get up and continue.

If you follow the journey of the labyrinth, the first two rounds seem to lead us away from the center, often like the first stages of our lives, we lose both the power of our soul and the knowing that directs us. The center can be misperceived as

The Journey

lying in this visible world of particular places, things, people or even states of being which need to be acquired. Be very mindful of what you want. If your want is to be loved, appreciated, and valued and that is your *true north*, your compass will gyrate endlessly, moving from one so-called true north to another. You will be ruled by the hunger for these things.

It's not about the destination, it's about the journey. This saying is about living in the moment. In the Medicine of One it would read, "The journey is the destination because the destination is the journey." Even if you don't know where something is going to lead you, if your intuitive compass is magnetized to the true north of who you are and the spine of your life, the journey becomes the destination. They are inseparable as you leap out of the *maze* and move toward the center of the *labyrinth*, which is the Circle. In this journey simplicity begins to rule.

Cultivate your presence on the journey as the true action of self-love, a compassion that delivers you to freedom ~ freedom through compassion, clearing the way to the center. As you journey through all the twists and turns of life anchor yourself in the great Circle it all moves in. The center is the feeling of flow, surrender, knowing, trust, confidence, and openness, protected not by a hard wall, but with your soft radiance. It is the *little you* that gets out of the way, so that life is simply done *through* you perfectly and not *by* you.

You must make the choice. *Do you want to live in the outer rings that are a maze of separation, mind, beliefs, materialism, greed, etc.? Or do you want to align with what your soul really wants ~ peace, truth, and beauty?*

The difficulty begins when we, as the little figure in the labyrinth pictured at the beginning of this chapter, forget we are the whole, and in that forgetting, our center seems lost, like something to be gained. In fact, the loss can be so painful we feel we can no longer go on in this state of separation. We feel helpless and powerless. To come to the center seems like a dream that is so far off and so unimaginable that we think, *why bother? Why continue?* We doubt and wonder if we are at the true entrance. *Maybe it's over here or over there.* The labyrinth becomes a maze as the thinking mind becomes dominant.

Medicine of One

If only I had. If only I hadn't. We all have moments in the journey when we reflect upon both pondered and split-second choices we made, and we believe if somehow they could be changed, or reversed the course of our life would have been greatly altered. Usually, we think, altered for the better. Experience is the stone sculptor's chisel. The deepest cuts are not when we get what we want, but rather when something unwanted crosses our path. Pain shapes us more than pleasure. Who wants change when everything feels good? Pain is often the jolt that thrusts us out of a state of complacency, but it can drive us into a corner of inertia and suffering if we run from it. When we run from pain that's when we hit the wall in the maze. This running is mirrored in the racing of the mind banging against the walls where there seems *no exit.*

The journey back to the center may require the *Gathering of Soul Medicine* and the transformation of imprisoned pain into a movement of life, a movement of music. This is the forward that may require gazing backward. All of your old bricks of pain hold within them the medicine of wholeness. Your greatest physician is *you* as the Medicine of One, as the Circle, and the remedies lay waiting within you.

It's time to grab the thread of the true self, which guides us out of the maze of the survivalist mind, and transform the maze into a labyrinth whose inward spiraling brings us home to the center where both maze and labyrinth are now a simple Circle of One. It's time to reclaim your *deep listening.*

Chapter Nine

The True Action of Self-Love
*The true action of self-love is aligning yourself
with who you really are. It's the beginning,
middle, and end of the Medicine of One.*

Come closer. Enter my world. Step into this Circle in the desert and stand with me. There is one thing above all others I want you to take from our time in the Circle ~ to deeply know the experience of self-love. If you grasp this and nothing else you have the key that unlocks the door through which everything else is revealed.

Self-love is not a thought. Because, if that is how you invoke it then you also invoke a war between an army of unloving thoughts and a peaceful corps of loving thoughts. If thinking is the problem, thinking won't free you. The true action of self-love cannot be a thought or something you say to yourself. The essence of the Circle is to mirror self-love as an actual feeling, breathing, expansive state of presence. It's a particular way of being present to all creation that moves within it.

Stand in the awareness of you here and now, and use your very breath as a tangible action to surrender to your own quiet, relaxed presence. The Medicine of One breath is an unbroken Circle of rhythmic flow. It's a unified intention that begins on the in-breath and completes itself in the fullness of the out-breath. And that surrendering sigh leads you into the next in-breath. What seems like in and out is more like something swinging back and forth, the pendulum of your *beingness*, which delivers it into the arms of the timeless One. The expansiveness of the in-breath is born from the surrender of the out-breath. You give everything up, everything you believe, every thought, and every ounce of history and give it to what has always been there, as if in the background like the sky is to the clouds. The more connected and present you become with the breathing, which begins with intent, the less you need to intend. Just feel yourself as if *being* breathed. It's like pulling back the bowstring ... and letting go ... and trusting that the arrow of surrender will lead you home into the mystery.

Lose everything but the feeling of *here,* and let that very *hereness* breathe you. Notice what happens to your breathing if you begin thinking. It becomes interrupted. What was unseparated appears to become separated. Return to the breath whose intention is surrender and attend to the fullness of the out-breath until even the in-breath has a quality of surrender. Stay there. Don't move. Sit in the center of the Circle as awareness that is presence. Do this ... nothing more. Come to know this spacious presence, and you come to know yourself as the love for all movements within the Circle. The true action of self-love is aligning yourself with who you really are. It's the beginning, middle, and end of the Medicine of One.

The Medicine of One is an undifferentiated extension of compassion that ripples from the deep well of yourself through every physical, emotional, mental, and spiritual tissue without limit into the world. True compassion must begin with yourself as the liberation of a radiance that is who you really are. You can call it love if you like, but this is just another concept. The thought or the words spoken are not these vibrant ripples that hold no judgment. They are not the *true action of self-love.* This compassion moves in your very breath, the breath of the Circle.

The idea of self-love is an old idea. But how do you go beyond the idea or the concept? You can't use the same mind that has been unloving to your inner life, and even hateful of some of its movements, to generate self-love. *The thinking mind divides. The still mind unites.*

If you get involved in all the conversations in your head that defend one side of an event then you invoke the oth-

The True Action of Self-Love

er side. If you have regret for not having done something, then these thoughts about what you should have done will be countered with other thoughts that you did all you could. Whichever side you get involved in invokes the other side. All of them are just *spins* of emotions entangled with thinking in the Circle.

The mind tries to control emotional movements. So a war is set in place between mind and emotion, and you are sucked into these movements back and forth. These movements are like the spin of a mouse on a wheel, driven by unliberated emotions and beliefs, and whipped on by thoughts born from the false perceptions of what is happening in your world. This is why you must give up the majority of your thinking to free them. It is not about the complete absence of thoughts. It's about **not** following them, not getting involved in them because to do so energizes the beliefs they embody and the emotions, which are driving them. It's like pouring gasoline on a fire.

What needs to happen is for you to not believe what the spins *think*. You must give up the beliefs holding it together. But at the same time the unmoved emotions that have not been honored are gathered back into the Circle of your *loving present here*, and allowed to move through your body with the aid of your *Honoring Breath* without restriction and without force. This is the *true action of self-love*.

The Many Voices

Daisy had been clinically diagnosed with dissociative identity disorder (multiple personality disorder). She was very functional and came to me with an earnest desire to have peace and wholeness. We walked along an area of the Verde River I call Rock Heaven because of the endless colors, texture, and types of rock. All the rocks had journeyed a long way down the river of life. But no two were same. Many of them began as bigger rocks that split apart and went on separate journeys. Imagine this splitting happening many times in the effort to survive the times when floodwaters roared through the canyons and carried those rocks great distances. Sometimes the rocks were buried at the bottom for years until massive movements of water forced them back to the surface. Each tumbled and spun until finally, swept so far from the river, they lay amongst millions of other rocks and boulders.

Imagine these broken rocks as the split off energy of a person who struggles through one trauma after another. In an effort to survive, they dissociate from the painful emotions in each experience. The person who begins the journey through life as one *whole* personality is divided into many parts just like pieces of broken rocks. These many voices (personalities) of the split off parts carry the charge of disowned emotions. Some of the voices rule and become dominant over the others, because they are formed in moments of survival. Other voices hold feelings that are such a *threat* to the survivalist controlling force they rarely get to appear and be heard. They are held captive and buried at the dark bottom of the river of life for years. Just like in real life, when people are imprisoned for beliefs, which threaten the status quo, the protector controller, the false ruler of their Circle is afraid of these *unvoiced feelings* until a new force of awareness begins to awaken. It is a force that does not rule, but rather blesses and honors. It is a compassionate light, which brings the lost ones to the shores of wisdom to be seen and loved.

I asked Daisy to gather all her personalities. She knew all of them because she had been in therapy for many years. She wandered along the riverbank taking her time and allowing the rocks to speak to her. My dogs Cheyenne and Shaman sat with me quietly in the shade as we waited for her. When she returned she was carrying five large rocks in her arms. I could see the weight was a strain. I asked her to put them in the truck and told her we were now going to the Circle. As we drove down the dirt road, I suggested that Daisy hold the rocks in her arms as if she were holding something fragile that needed caring attention. When I stopped the truck and turned the engine off, I handed her a leather bag to carry the rocks to the Circle, which was a ten-minute walk through scrub brush, juniper, and Palo Verde trees.

At one point we had to walk up an incline to the top of a mesa and I said to her, "I want you to feel this weight you are carrying, and have this sense as you walk that you are bringing

The True Action of Self-Love

all these children that are within to their home in the Circle. Really *feel* that this moment has been waiting for you and when you enter the Circle, you enter this moment."

She nodded and smiled at me. At that moment a hawk flew over us and screeched. We both stopped and looked at it circling. Neither of us needed to say anything. A soft smile flowed between us.

Shaman and Cheyenne had already trotted ahead to the Circle after chasing a cottontail rabbit that eluded them. They were sitting in the shade of a Palo Verde tree that stood outside the Circle when we arrived.

I asked Daisy to set the bag down. There was a center rock that was about three feet in circumference and rose out of the ground five inches. In the center I had carved a small hole. In that hole a beautiful white rock that resembled both a human heart and a mother holding a child sat in an upright position. I picked it up and said, "The center of the Circle is the heart of a mother's unconditional love. It's vast and spreads to the horizon. There is a power and energy here. Let it support you. Bring your bag into the Circle, Daisy, and just set it down."

Daisy did as I asked, set the bag down and said, "It feels good here. Peaceful ... and so quiet."

"Yes," I replied. "That peace and quiet is who you really are and these children in your bag were separated from that peace because you were trying to survive. Your emotions and feelings became divided, cast into the dark but dwelling alone in different caves. From this division *the many* were born, and you forgot the *one* they all move in. You have gathered the many and they all get to be here ... all of them ... because nothing gets thrown out of the Circle. And remember, Daisy, you *are* the Circle. You are what they move in, a loving compassionate presence. Reach into your bag and trust that your hand will touch the right one to bring into this spacious love."

Daisy slowly reached into the black leather bag and drew out a black volcanic rock the size of her fist and pitted with holes, and spoke, "It's the me penetrated by my dad that swore vengeance. I remember the moment it came in to protect me. It was after many years of helpless abuse. When it came in it shouted, 'Touch me again, and I will tell everybody.

Medicine of One

Touch me again and I will kill you!'"

I asked Daisy to breathe and relax, to feel that peace and quiet she had commented on when first arriving. She stood quietly for a moment. "Let it be like an affectionate awareness to that hard anger of protection. Give yourself permission to have the feeling of hate, knowing it comes from great hurt." I put my hands on her shoulders to encourage them to drop and let go. First I asked her to lie on her back, stiff and helpless, as if her father were lying on top of her. She started to cry and shake. At first it was intense and wanted to go on forever. I said, "Be the Circle to it ... sigh ... relax ... give your body to the earth ... breathe. Love this little one."

After ten seconds of whimpering and crying, her breathing calmed and she lay still. I asked, "How do you feel?"

"I feel less anxious, more relaxed, more like ... me. Like there *is* a *me*."

"Reach in the bag and take out this little fragile one."

She let her hand grope in the dark as if knowing what she was searching for. She pulled out a little heart rock the size of her fingernail and started crying again.

I spoke softly, "Although the first rock you pulled out was your rage, the key to its freedom is this *fragile little one*. Of all these many voices in the dark it's the one that is the most deeply buried because it is utterly defenseless and powerless. You have touched it and by letting it just move through your body without being owned by its story you have freed it with your own compassion. Remember this feeling because it is the true action of self-love and it's the force that will unite everyone."

I asked her to hold the rock and go back to the stiff helpless place. She did and now there were only a few tears. Then I directed her to leap to her feet and with her whole body point her finger at the perpetrator and scream, "Touch me again and I will kill you!" Then I said, "Breathe ... relax ... just let it go everywhere. Just be what's aware of your tears and let them move." The feelings trembled through her in seconds and I could see her filling up with a new strength and confidence.

"Yes," I said. "These two were separated. We have

The True Action of Self-Love

blended them back together again by invoking these two opposite feelings."

She laughed and cried, "I'm here, I'm back ... I'm home."

And then I said, "And that home is your own compassionate presence as the Circle of One."

The remaining rocks in the bag were now easily brought into the Circle through honoring very specific feelings. Each rock held a different feeling. Each rock brought her another step into wholeness. Each rock liberated and served the greater Circle of who she was.

It takes no leap of the imagination to understand how Daisy's split off energies can mirror all of us in our journey through life. In surviving we cultivate a habit of suppression and rejection, of trying to throw the *undesirable ones* out of the Circle. We think, *if I can get rid of this I will have peace.* But the opposite becomes true and the many voices clamor for attention inside of us. You can't just set up another war between the *you* who wants peace and quiet and all the other members of the Circle who are voicing their chorus of wants. You can't gag them and expect to have peace. You can't throw them out of the Circle because if the Circle, the Medicine of One, is limitless, how could anything possibly be thrown out of it? The root of the problem is *you* trying to throw things out. *What you resist you become.*

I have used Daisy's story as an example of the reintegration of the past experiences. What about now? What about day-to-day life that presents us with pain and challenges such as chronic physical pain, an ongoing financial problem, or a life-threatening crisis with yourself or a loved one? This is why I consider the Medicine of One a path, not a process or a method. It's a way of moving through each moment of life as the Circle and as the true action of self-love.

My own life and challenges are my greatest teachers. I learn much from working with others, but my own intimate, immediate experience, and my earnest commitment to be present with it is by far my greatest teacher. Very often when I stand in the Circle with someone I try to share something from my own life if I can. I want us to stand on the same ground and

I want them to know that just because I am in the position of helping them doesn't mean I don't face my own challenges.

Soft Love of the Warrior

Each day I begin by sitting in the Circle. This first Circle of the day is in front of my fireplace. I light a small fire and a candle. But this sitting is different than the *do nothing/be quiet* sitting in the Circles on the land, for this sitting allows me to function for a portion of the day.

When I flipped the Healy and hit the pavement, instinctual movements did everything possible to preserve my life. The coiling away from the impact entered all the tissues of my body. Six months after the accident, I began to notice pressure on the sides of my skull. Immediately upon returning to California I seemed to be in a bit of a daze. I had a cabin in the Santa Cruz Mountains and I would just go out on the deck and stare at the redwood trees and sky for hours. It wasn't until seven years later that a chiropractor pointed out that my right shoulder, the part of my body that hit the pavement with the greatest force, was significantly higher than my left. Some time later I explored other modalities and learned that my head had been driven and twisted to the middle of my back.

I began to wonder if many of the problems I was having for much of that time were the result of that defining moment on I-70. These cognitive, emotional, and physical difficulties made each day a hellish journey. I felt like Sisyphus, who was condemned for an eternity by the Greek gods and as punishment was forced to push a huge boulder to the top of a hill only to have it roll back down.

Prior to beginning this book, I would begin each day by assuming a full lotus position, reaching out as if grabbing a ball, drawing my hands in a couple of inches from my mouth, my elbows parallel with my arm pits, feeling my skull as if it were being pulled from the base ... feeling and envisioning my skull, neck, chest, and shoulders opening.

As of the writing of this new second edition of *Medicine of One* in 2013, that which used to work and offer a reprieve ... stopped working. That which gave me the feeling of a measure of control ... disappeared. So, please know that I speak from the trenches, not from the safety and comfort of the

The True Action of Self-Love

pulpit. Daily I walk this path I am sharing.

It took me a span of twenty years to discover that position. If I didn't do it, I was fairly dysfunctional, cognitively, emotionally, and physically. More often than not, there were adverse consequences when not done perfectly right. Within this story is the dilemma ~ the balance between *action* and *surrender.* This can be one of the most difficult and delicate parts of *the path* to walk. This is the drawing back of the arrow, a tension that is tensionless, and releasing it to find the target rather than driving it willfully to the target.

With my physical dilemma, doing nothing would leave me almost incapacitated. But doing too much would lead to the same state of imbalance. The balance between surrender and action was to enter the form and yet surrender into it ... to take the step forward, so to speak, and surrender to where it would lead me ... to create without control. This kind of surrender does not give in to defeatist thoughts, but neither does it let the tough warrior take over and push. Yet, the strength of the warrior is invoked. So it's really about rooting yourself in the soft love of the Medicine of One, where warrior and victim are honored, felt, and transformed into a mutual ground of support.

All of us face difficulties in some form or another. Some of these are the result of experiences from the past, and there are those in the present that are experienced *through* the past. Either one holds the potential of suffering if we are the victim, if we let them own us, drawing us into a kind of vortex of fearful thinking and emotional disturbance. But the detachment of the warrior cowboy who dusts his jeans off and walks away won't work either. For in doing this, we are really turning our Circle over to the preservation of how we define ourselves, at any expense. The price is *true* peace. The Medicine is the t*rue action of self-love.*

Some days I am weary to the bone. There is a voice in the Circle mumbling softly, "I am tired, I can't do it anymore." There is a feeling of hopelessness. If I just ignore it and push on ... push it out ... harden to it ... yes, I will get through to the next day. But, the habitual rejection of these weaker, sometimes helpless, movements in the Circle of *Who I Am* creates a kind of spinning black hole that haunts me with moments of suffering.

And so I must learn what it means to love them, to be the open spacious Circle of *no judgment* and allow that desperate energy to ripple through my body as a heavy dark wave that rolls forward into completion as a cycle of life that emerges as a hopeful *surrender*. Not a *surrender* to a victim's thinking, but rather a *surrender* that in its spaciousness allows me to settle to my ground of being and trust. Yes, a *surrender* that trusts the truth of *Who I Am*. This is the true *action* of self-love.

Each day I commit myself to this and perhaps, in the eyes of the ever present critic, I fail. So let me love this critic and let me love this failure. Let me remember the infinite *One that I Am* in my weakest distraught moments and let the bed I lay my weary self upon be that Medicine of One.

If you can actually be the Circle to your own willful self-criticism and judgment, then its unloving appearance means nothing. It does not mean that you cannot love yourself. This true action holds no judgment, even with the force in you that might feel compelled to judge yourself and others. It is a detachment that is spaciously all-inclusive and not a detachment of moving away from your emotional being. All movements are honored. There are no rules except one ~ *harmlessness*. To honor something as potentially damaging as rage is not a license to behave recklessly; nor is it a license to put this energy into the world. It is to be spacious to the pain from which it was born, and transform the frozen fire into something that gifts the world with the flame of creation.

I, too, am human. I, too, forget. I, too, feel the grip of fear. I, too, in forgetting, wrap my painful emotions in robes of spiritual thought, mistaking that high thought for the Medicine. I, too, want relief from my pain. So let me just love them all, every movement in this infinite, spacious, compassionate Circle of this great mystery that I Am. Let me be this Medicine of One as the *true action of self-love*.

Chapter Ten

The True Sun

*Ask yourself in a moment of suffering,
"What am I believing that has brought me here?"*

I will share with you my own personal *world*, my world of difficulties, my world of pain and challenges. Too often we read the teachings of others and feel that we are far beneath them. We actually use these *enlightened* teachings to belittle ourselves into hopelessness. We read the words of these *knowledgeable* ones, and it seems they never behaved harmfully toward themselves or others. We make ourselves feel far behind, empty, and utterly hopeless because "we're not as enlightened." We do this by comparing the deprecated view of ourselves to whom we have imagined the *enlightened ones* to be. So I use myself and stand on the same ground with you because when you are at the bottom of a pit, it's easy to feel there is no way out. I am a man, incarcerated in the same prison as many, who found a *way* out. I am sharing that pathway out. The door is there, waiting for the *key of your compassion.*

I have journeyed in the underworld of this life. My passage through the darkness bordered on a kind of self-annihilating, demonic, Lucifer-like daring to tread on the edge of insanity without losing that sanity. I lived in the age of LSD dropped into the corneas of eyes. With the amphetamine-like hunger of LSD I could consume infinite alcohol and still remain stoically sober. I know what it is like to drink and drug myself into oblivion not once, but many, many times, until I lay like a crippled bird at the bottom of a deep shaft looking up at an orb of light above me. I know this inability to save one's self. I know the moment of being brought to my knees in prayer for help. I prayed to what I did not know. I had no other choice. This prayer was a call for help that opened the door within so that I might receive the shining rays of the sun of my true self.

With hopelessness can come the inability to have faith … to have that one single belief that who we really are is the *quiet presence of compassion and peace*. In the depths of despair there is a stubbornness, which can take root. In that isolated stubbornness we cannot seek the *life giving water of help*. The words that form a plea for help cannot touch our lips. The need to be strong and independent can block the way. When we are so anchored in this stubbornness we close the door to the help of our true self, our true peace. The pathway to peace is to be compassion to the *unpeaceful*.

Right now there is someone sleeping in one of my sacred Circles. Her name is Sandra. There has been a belief lurking in the dark, which has always tightened around her pain. It's the belief that *there is something wrong with me* and it is the anchor for all the stories in her life. When I directed her into her need for love and companionship, this tight belief turned the simple feeling of *I want to be loved* into the suffering belief of *I will never be loved.* The first phrase is just a feeling that must be brought into the Circle of compassion. The second is a belief that blocks the way to movement … a belief that has become her *truth*.

The next day when I went to the Circle to see how I could serve her, she had done a lot more work with herself *clearing the way*. One of the chores I had left her with was digging up some large rocks in the Circle that had become exposed by the wind. She showed me several large boulder sized rocks she had dug up and put in the Circle. Then she had filled in the empty holes left behind with soft soil. She'd had many "Aha!" *moments* since the previous day, but this was her last day and a kind of gloomy angst had settled in. She told me that here in this Circle, and with me, was the only time she didn't feel alone. Here was the feeling of *home* that once again she had to leave behind.

As we stood looking off into the distance, we could see

The True Sun

the red mountains with rolling, buff colored soil, dotted with green shrubs and yellow flowers. They were shrouded in a great blanket of smoke from a large fire burning 20 miles away. Fire destroys and kills. But this fire of destruction is natural and fertilizes the soil for new growth. The ponderosa pine where the fire was burning needed a fire to regenerate. So, too, the fire of Sandra's grief needed to be allowed to burn a dark path through the beauty of what dies. In order for the sun to once again rise, it must disappear to come again another day. That burning, dark path is our pain. But the dark leads to the dawning light.

Sandra did not want to say goodbye to what she loved. In this moment it was the land and our spiritual friendship. But back where she lived, her best friend was dying of cancer. In fact, her whole life had been frozen in that moment of refusal to let what she loved slip from her hands. This grip was the tension that could not bear to utter the final goodbye. She had been frozen in this space for an eternity, as if life after life. It was as though that dark path of loss's pain had burned straight down into her core and it lay there smoldering because of her refusal to give it the compassionate soft breath that would allow it to complete its movement. Yet, without realizing it she had already symbolically initiated living this story differently than ever before. She had already invoked how I would finally serve her. Once she dug up the rock of her unmoved grief, exposed it, and completed her actions by placing the soft soil of compassion in the *empty hole* of the *grave*, she altered what she had taken to be her destiny ~ to be alone and to always suffer in her losses.

I walked over to the big boulder she had dug up, lifted it, dropped it in the Circle and said, "This is the gravestone. It's time." She started weeping. She was standing above it and I asked her to kneel before it, as if kneeling with the finality of the moment of placing a dead body in the ground and covering it with dirt.

She hesitated and tensed, her body speaking, "I don't want to." I had her honor that "I don't want to" by saying it and consciously tensing. Now she was able to kneel before the gravestone.

Medicine of One

I shared a story she already knew about the death of my dogs and in particular the most recent death of Hanta Yo. I told her his body was there before me. I knew I had to bury him to give my grief the boundlessness it needed. I told her about the song I always sang at the moment of pulling the dirt on the body. I asked her if she knew a song that would be right for this moment.

"Ave Maria," she said.

"Sing it with the love of goodbye," I said.

"No. I can't," she replied.

"Why?"

"I can't sing."

"You don't have a choice. The body needs to be laid in the ground, just like Hanta Yo. I didn't have a choice. You have been kneeling before this gravestone for an eternity, unable to sing. It's time. You don't have a choice. You have to."

She began to sing and weep. As she sang, I asked her to see her good friend who was dying of cancer. For ten seconds her grief rolled through her and then it was quiet. She wrapped the stone with a ribbon and a feather. The gloomy angst was gone. She had brought the sun of her true self into the dark empty room of loss and grief. Now the forest of life within her could regenerate with new loves, new friends, and new places called *home*. Magically, the smoke in the sky was beginning to lift and it looked like it would rain soon. By completing her final gesture of grief, Sandra could now receive the *blessed rain from the sky*. Something had moved so the sunrays of her true self that had been within her eternally could pierce the dark clouds that had covered the sky.

The sun is always there shining in the heavens even on the darkest night or the stormiest day. Even in the painfully empty, dark periods in our life this *sun of our true self* is there, always shining. Its warmth and light seem to disappear when we align ourselves with our story's pain and beliefs. It's as if the door opening to this sun to our true self is closed. Our life can feel like a dark, empty room where we wait for the light to come from without. But we are the creator of the door that blocks the shining of our truth and peace that is within. The weight pressing against the door is our own mind preventing

The True Sun

the door from opening. Take the belief away and there is no weight. Ask yourself in a moment of suffering, "What am I believing that has brought me here? What would be different if I just choose not to believe it?"

Darkness and light, empty and full, alternate in our lives, but we are the shining presence that persists through the whole cycle. There is no other source of light to fill the room of your life. We are the life-giving sun, which fills the room with peaceful warmth.

No matter how bad it gets, the way out is right there within, without, and all around you. Take what feels like your last breath, and in that moment make a different choice. In that moment let the breath of life come back into you like an answer to your final prayer. Simply choose to no longer believe your mind.

Medicine of One

Chapter Eleven

Freedom Through Compassion
Compassion is freedom no matter where you are.

Great people like Nelson Mandela have found freedom within physical prisons they could not escape. They were able to cultivate compassionate love for those who imprisoned them even while still incarcerated. They found a Circle of self-compassion within the small dark space of their prison. It's as if on the floor of their cell they drew a Circle of compassion in the dust and committed themselves to it. They took up the heart and this became the center ~ this heart that is the true, quiet, present, peaceful awareness that we are.

The feeling of being trapped invokes our instincts of survival. We think and tense, push, shove and struggle ... gritting our teeth. We want to be free, but trap ourselves in a web of our own making. In our humanness we want something beyond just surviving. We want peace and happiness, which are the sisters and brothers of freedom.

You could be trapped in a job you don't like, or the place you live, a house, city, landscape, or country, and at the moment you just have to be with it. The circumstance of your prison might be a marriage or a relationship that is simply not going to change regardless of how hard you have tried to change it.

Perhaps you feel trapped in your body, unable to be free of constant pain or a physical disability unable to get out of bed, go outside, or move about without a wheelchair. You don't have to be a person who is extremely independent to feel the *fragileness* of this moment, to feel the loss of control of your world, to feel imprisoned by your very body when there is no escape.

There are many circumstances in life in which you can't just walk out the cell door. You can't. And your feelings of *limitation, being trapped, loss of control, helplessness,* and *powerlessness* are sitting there inside of you all the time. Your *victim* feelings become very energized in all these stories and you hate these feelings. You want to get rid of them. You want to be free of your suffering thoughts and whatever you are trapped *in* seems to be the source of your suffering. But it is really your relationship to what you are trapped in and all the feelings that it engenders, which have created your prison.

If you are suffering you will more than likely feel imprisoned as if there is no way out. No matter what the circumstance you can feel trapped and unable to change it. This *imprisonment* intensifies because you are trying to get out by the same habits that built the walls. *Get rid of the feelings. Control them and don't let them move.* The feelings are still seen as the enemy, and the events or people that set them in motion are seen as the cause.

We do whatever we have to do from our instinctual need to survive. We do what *seems to work* at making us feel safe and able to go on *surviving.* We develop a habit in relationship to our emotional being. We develop the habit of suppression and denial to *get rid of* the closest thing that causes us pain and disturbance, the one thing we seem to be able to control ~ our emotions. We control them with the force of our minds which then enlists the body to serve its goal ~ protection. We try to protect our value, safety, and power by controlling the emotions when these things are threatened. We can't control what other people do, so we try to control the feelings set in motion by other people's actions and behavior toward us by not allowing our feelings to move and by withholding breath ... life.

We build a fortress so people and experience cannot hurt us. This works too well. Our fortress becomes a prison that is built from suppression and oppression, control, and the immobilization of emotional movements. These are the oppo-

Freedom Through Compassion

site of self-compassion and lead to being unaware of what is moving inside of you. We are safe from having to feel the threats from without, but now we are separated not only from others but also inevitably from the true Circle of the presence that we are. We are safe but disconnected from ourselves and separated from others. Next to our physical body our emotions are our most immediate experience. Our *deep presence* lives in this *now* and so our very emotions are a doorway to our *true self*.

This feeling of separation is created and held in place by your own mind. The mind has petrified these moments of feeling in the cement of fear. Petrified has a dual meaning: a fear in which you are unable to move, and the solidifying of organic material into a concrete substance. Your soul's energy becomes trapped in this wall that defends and protects you from the pain you did not want to feel because it seemed impossible to both survive and feel at the same time. Now this great citadel of survival is a sterile, lifeless prison, and the *feeling* of being trapped, helpless, not in control, and cut off becomes so unbearable that what used to allow us to survive now chokes us to death. We are caught in the maze of the mind with seemingly no way out.

The stones of the fortress walls are our unmoved emotions and the mortar a willful, controlling mind that adopts righteous beliefs: *righteous* meaning simply, *I'm right*. This is not the true nature of the mind. The mind is not the enemy. Thinking is only one action of the mind. The mind turned outward to the world and used to control is the creator of suffering. Suffering is really the tightening grip around the feeling, because the result is intensification. Most people don't *try* to cry. They try *not* to cry, which only intensifies it.

We learn quickly as we grow up that our mind is our greatest ally in our effort to survive. But this allegiance is as a protecting, controlling force, which creates endless fearful thinking. A vicious cycle has been created. The walls that protect you imprison you, and from this separated disconnected place you create life circumstances in which you can feel trapped.

Freedom is gained through the reversal of your life-

Medicine of One

time habit of how you use your mind. Now, in this moment, as you read these words you can choose to live differently to free yourself from these stories of suffering. This freedom is realized through your own compassion to the emotional movements you have been unloving to in the vastness of your soul's experience.

You can choose to *be* that Circle, to soften and relax to the feelings of the victim without believing in its thinking and to soften and breathe into the fear that can drive the warrior to build the strongest most impenetrable walls. Do not let your history and your stories become, or continue to be, the walls of your prison. Clear the way with the *true action of self-love*.

Your gentle awareness is a light you shine on the *stone wall* of your unmoved emotional history and beliefs. The Medicine of One is about the invocation of this presence and compassion to gently and lovingly dissolve the wall by the simple act of living life in a different way. The mind turned inward toward itself *is* the *Self*, the presence of you as the Circle. This presence is naturally compassionate to all things that move within it.

Living the path of the Circle is simply reversing your habit of controlling your emotional being and aligning yourself with your great, compassionate true self and moving through life that way. You don't have to try to *be* compassion ~ it's your *truth of self*.

This experience and situation of being trapped can be used as a challenge to compassionately engage whatever feelings are set in motion. Invoke your Circle of compassion to all the feelings that are moving ~ feelings, not thoughts. The walls are the *stones of unmoved emotion* suppressed and cemented there. The thoughts are the bars of the prison. The prison is what you decide to make it, even if it's a real prison. So even in a prison there is the possibility of freedom. The bars of the prison are what you believe. What do *you* believe? Surrender these beliefs to the compassion of the Circle. Believe one thing ~ you *are* this *compassion*. Now you must discover what that actually feels like in the *true action of self-love*.

Because we think so much we tend to localize the experience of ourselves in our skull and even the rest of our body

Freedom Through Compassion

becomes an object to us, which we view from this boney structure where the brain is. You, your presence, is not located in your skull, nor trapped there. Even if you have the belief that you are anchored in the heart, the true *heart self* does not have a physical home in this organ. It's all around and through you as consciousness. Don't limit it. Adopt a new possibility that your personal Circle is ultimately connected to everything, Circles within Circles on into infinity. Just let it be possible. Let it be possible that your notion of God is not something separate, but that you are inseparable and part of a continuity of God, like a drop of water in the ocean. When that particle of water stirs it ripples on into infinity.

Draw a Circle around you, either literally in the dirt or with your mind, or put a rope or string out to give you the feel of it. Put your attention in front of you ... in back of you ... to your left ... and to your right ... above ... and below ... and finally ... and most importantly ... behind you. Sensing the space behind immediately relaxes your eyes and allows them to give up focusing directly on what is in front of them. You are invoking your peripheral vision, which allows you to feel the space behind you. This is an aid to help you enter an expanded state of heightened awareness. Feel as if you are in a stalking mode, like a hunter stalking its prey. But you are stalking with love, with compassion. You are sensing beyond the limits of your body. You are removing the limiting belief that who you are is this body.

Through daily compassion for yourself you are freeing the energies that have anchored you into that story. As the old charge dissipates you can stop believing what you think within that story and let the story dissolve into the Circle and enliven it with freed energies. Whether it's the story of the victim, the story of the warrior, the story of abuse, the story of an accident, the story of poverty or the story of a prison, energies once trapped are now liberated.

I don't know what the future holds for you or myself. Our bodies may suffer limitations that come to it through the soul's need to experience those limitations. No matter what difficulty or pain moves in your Circle, the Medicine of One is a path, which invites you to meet your own pain in a new way.

Medicine of One

It is not a formula for having a painless life, but a path to a life of peace in spite of pain.

The Medicine of One uses the Circle on many levels to help you step compassionately beyond defining yourself as your body, emotions, mind, or any other system that would separate the presence that you are into parts; even the notions of spirit and soul. All these labels help us map things out so we can talk about this human experience and try to understand it. This Circle is a way of describing your deepest self. Oneness is you as that Circle. Compassion is you as that Circle. It is a presence you can feel.

The Circle of you is there no matter where you are, even in extreme circumstances. Even if you are sitting in prison and cannot see the sky, you can become the sky. You can become spaciousness. You can be compassion to yourself ~ compassion to your fear, compassion to your hate, compassion to your rage, compassion to your grief. The Circle *is* compassion. It begins as self-compassion and leads you back home to the center. This compassion is the way to freedom no matter where you are.

Chapter Twelve

Loving the Hungry Ghost
*The true cradle the infant within
hungers for must be the arms invoked
by our own presence as the Circle*

An infant girl named Mary was born into the frequency of being a mistake ~ something unwanted. Her mother told her from infancy she was unwanted and a nuisance. Her father loved her. In fact, he loved her more than he loved his wife, her mother. So added to this unwanted vibration was the vibration of the mother's jealousy. As a child Mary needed attention, diapers changed, food, and blankets to keep out the cold. Just to receive the bare essentials she had to be attended to. She couldn't feed and clothe herself. Her mother resented this; before this child, Mary, came along, she was the center of attention. She had better things to do like shopping and hanging out at the bar with her friends. Now all the attention had to go to this infant.

Mary's father doted over his little girl. But her father held her ... closer and closer. Consumed by his own hungry needs, one night he entered her bedroom and gave her the attention she craved, soft, nurturing, and adoring. *He likes me ... he loves me*, she thought. Although she sensed a *wrongness* to it all, Mary's *hungry ghost* was calmed.

A pattern began and continued year after year until she perceived there was truly no love coming from him, only desire, and she was the *object* of his desire. She was not something valued or protected. No one had ever protected her. Nor had her sense of self been nurtured. She wondered, *why am I not worth caring for and protecting?* This question became ever present in her life. The doubt of worth sat within in her like a worm in an apple, gnawing at her sense of self.

The paradox is that Mary sought love from outside of herself that could not come from without. What she sought was a sense of self, built on a foundation made of the *attention of others*. Why? Because, she never had a healthy opportunity to experience her natural, healthy, beautiful, *little* i*/me*. This pursuit takes her further away from the center of the Circle of self and deeper into the maze of the hungry ghost.

The true simplicity of our journey through the labyrinth can be thwarted in our infancy. Deprived of the essential need to feel loved, we become destined for the maze of the hungry ghost. I use the term *hungry ghost* to name something inside of us hungering for the essentials of life and who we are, peace and love. This true desire becomes hijacked through the deprivation of love. This hunger is in direct proportion to the degree of our starvation in infancy and childhood. This starvation can be for basic needs of food, warmth, and protection. These are all given when love is present. But they can also be given without love, without warmth, without true caring.

As that child, when the natural expression of love towards us through touch, words, and a look in the eyes is not given and even withheld to control our behavior, something begins to undermine our healthy feeling of existence. This healthy feeling of existence is experienced through being seen, heard, and held with unconditional love. The absence of this creates an absence within, an emptiness that hungers for the loving attention not given and the doubt of selfhood. We hunger to be loved as that child in various critical moments, or we hunger because it was an ongoing environment where we did not feel loved.

Imagine yourself as an infant in a crib. You reach out to be held and no one is *there*. You are left in the dark. It's cold and there are disturbing noises. You are frightened, and no one is *there*, only the feeling of cold and dark, the opposite of what you want. Another time you make your first attempt to stand

Loving the Hungry Ghost

and if someone was just *there,* attentive to your first effort, it would happen. You would share the moment with warmth. But when you try to stand, there is no one *there*. Or when they were there and you made the attempt they laughed when you fell. Your intense wanting is created because there is no one there as a loving, spacious Circle of safety and support for healthy emotional growth. *No one there* means now you hunger for someone, as a loving compassionate presence, to *be there.* The outstretched arms of the infant linger on into adulthood seeking to fill the emptiness within through a specific kind of attention from without.

Deprived of love, the drive to find that love gains intensity similar to other instinctual drives around our basic needs of food, shelter, and water. Love is truly a basic need although we can live without it.

The concept of the hungry ghost comes from many of the Far Eastern religious and folk lore including China, Japan, and India, where it is depicted in artwork as being half beast and half human because of this subhuman instinctual drive. Their necks, throats, and mouths are disproportionally small compared to their great bulging hungry stomachs. This disproportion reveals the relationship between the excess of their hunger and their ability to receive love. Their small mouths and throats means the favorable attention, which comes to them, is never enough. As a result, their hunger is insatiable.

The hungry ghost is created through the deprivation of one's basic needs. That deprivation sets emotions into movement the person does not want to feel because these emotions take them back to the *cold, dark, empty* place. Those feelings *haunt* them with unworthiness and doubt, which, if fed with the desired attention makes them feel good, makes them feel loved. The feelings of protection, value, and safety give temporary peace, but the peace is a false peace because true, permanent peace flowers from your own *true action of self-love.*

The hunger for love is truly the hunger for the *feeling of identity.* If there is a hungry ghost within someone, being alone can hurl them into nothingness. They want the love they did not experience as a child. Their hungry ghost hungers for it. They may move through life falsely interpreting much of their experience as a threat to their value, power, and safety ~ a threat to their fragile identity. It's even more difficult for them when they are cut off from knowing the nature of their wanting and unaware that the source is within themselves. It's always others who hurt them and deny them what they need. Or they might be aware of their hungry ghost but unable to prevent it from seeking out what it wants and the feelings of the original deprivation are triggered. The feelings are triggered as they view the world through the lens of their old pain, perceive the intent of an action, and react to it. They perceive that something is being purposely withheld from them, which only intensifies their need.

If there is someone in your life you love and they die, who dies? The one you love or the one who loves you? If it's *the one who loves you,* your world will disappear because now the one who gave you loving attention and value is gone. In the absence of this *given value* a great vacancy of your worth is created. The mistake here is that your experience of *Self* came from outside you. This feeling of worthy presence was given to you through a particular kind of attention. What is given can be lost or taken away. On an unconscious level the question "Who am I?" has been answered by "I am the one who is loved. Without love I am nothing, nobody." When the person who loved you is gone, everything can seem to vanish with them, value, worth, feelings of safety, and security, and ultimately your identity and place in the world ... or so you think and feel.

It may be true this thing called **i** is an illusion. But the pain of many is that there is no substance to their **i**-ness. This no **i** is in fact an **i** with a story. It's an **i** that is like an empty shell. It's an **i** that hangs on to the story of deprivation; it lacks the *presence of here,* the **I** *am here.* It hungers for that. Too much soul energy has been both *stolen from them* and *rejected by them*, and the consciousness cannot inhabit the body. The experience of many is that something has been lost, which is the source of true connection and peace.

Without this confident *hereness,* the way back home beyond this little **i** to the big **I** is almost impossible. The dilemma and the paradox is the great hungry ghost yearns for

Loving the Hungry Ghost

the confidence present in a healthy feeling of identity. Many forms of spirituality ask you to be willing to give up being polarized in this identity as the truth of who you are. In the Medicine of One you surrender this little **i** to the big **I** that stands in the center of the Circle of One. You surrender through the *true action of self-love* ~ not by an act of will, but by an act of love. But how can you surrender an identity you don't have, which is dependent on the attention of others? You can't. Your first act of true self-love is the engagement of your hungry ghost by consciously choosing to bring it into the greater Circle of you. Your own awakening awareness is the sword of truth that cuts through the walls of the maze until you stand face to face with the fragile little **i**. This abandoned little one is the core of powerlessness and helplessness that can hide in the form of an angry hungry ghost.

Many of the people who come to me have had great trauma in their childhood, and all have had difficulties that block the way home. The Medicine of One was born from my work with people having difficult or traumatic stories for which the teaching of *being here now* is impossible. The way out of their own maze is a journey of clearing the way to the possibility, the certainty, and finally the reality of their own true presence.

The core desire is truly for peace even if it takes on the form of the desire to be loved. Somewhere within the maze many will encounter the hungry ghost. You can be trapped in the maze as a fighting warrior or a powerless victim. The way out of the maze is the same for both ~ the direct engagement of the hungry ghost. It is the true action of self-love, as we gaze into the wanting eyes of our own hunger with compassion. Self-love is the *hereness*, your *true presence,* from which value and confidence radiate effortlessly. This effortless radiance gives us the power to choose the path we walk, to behave from the place of *deep listening*, and to live the pure love of being.

The true cradle the infant within hungers for must be the arms invoked by our own presence as the Circle, like a great bird with the soft wings of self-compassion that gently rocks the infant's trembling feelings of helplessness and powerlessness into peace. Through this comforting motion the

Medicine of One

feelings discharge downward into the earth and we stand in the power of our true presence. We become the love we hungered for and are now the Circle where giving and receiving love are One.

Chapter Thirteen

The Warrior and the Victim

Challenge yourself to be the Circle to the victim and the warrior. Release the true strength of the warrior, and liberate the true compassion of the victim.

You may cringe at the word *victim* and admire the word *warrior*. The polarized warrior and the polarized victim are both entrenched in corners of the maze generated by an *old story*. Neither is the place to live from. They are both dots in the Circle that can own the Circle and spin everything into their worldview. Both the warrior's and the victim's survival tactics are defensive moves that keep them spinning in the maze, incapable of grasping the thread of their true self. Their habit of controlling never allows the trust of their *deep listening* that can follow the thread. Here they sit, safe but imprisoned, their true gifts to the world unliberated.

The *warrior* and the *victim* both live in a world where there is a feeling of perpetual threat to their safety, value, or power. Obviously there are circumstances where our physical safety is clearly being threatened. There is no interpretation or assumption involved that leads to a response. If a boulder is rolling toward you or someone is holding a gun on you, you must respond to save your life. The threat is real. What I am talking about is when a threat is perceived where there is none. If someone pushes their way in front of me in line at the grocery store, where is the threat? If someone says something to me that brings into question the integrity of my actions or diminishes the quality of my work or the value of what I have said, and I feel myself hardening, going numb, pulling away, getting angry, or feeling hurt ... what is really going on here? I experience threat because I already have within me a gnawing doubt. Without my own doubt there would be no threat.

If I am not living from the *center of the Circle of the truth of who I am,* but owned by my victim or warrior, then that is where I perceive and respond from, because that is the place from which I live. The warrior attacks and the victim shrinks. Both are defending. Both believe their perception of the situation is the truth. They believe they are right. So the real question here is what are you defending?

This is a good question to ask yourself repeatedly as you walk the path of self-knowledge and experience yourself in reaction to something that has happened. Why am I angry, hurt, numb, shut down, or hardening? What have I perceived through my *historical lens,* created from unintegrated emotions, and assumed has been threatened? The lenses of your perceptions are created from your old stories. These generate assumptions that ignite hated emotions and drive the spin of thinking. You believe these thoughts and you suffer.

What is *truly* real needs no defense. It simply *is.* So when you react in actions or spoken or written words, what has been threatened? What are you assuming has happened? What are you actually feeling? Beneath numb, cold, and withdrawn, is the hurt and the anger wrapped around the core of fear. It is very simple and needs no analysis*: I am angry and I am afraid.* But the key here is not just a *thought of self-acceptance*. In this way you stay in the mind. The *thought of acceptance* is not the *true action of self-love*, which engages the actual feelings of anger and fear as the Circle of compassion. *I am afraid* must be uttered vibrantly with a small voice echoing from its tomb in your pelvis, as you anchor yourself as the spacious Circle. This is freedom through self-compassion.

When we are children and we witness and suffer what would seem the unendurable, no one is helping us find our way. We either hide and shrink into the *victim*, completely cut off from the warrior within, or we polarize and harden into the *warrior*. It can happen in an instant ... in one defining moment. Enough! But then we stay in that place for the rest of our lives

The Warrior and the Victim

and perceive the world through the lens of our history. We all have stories that have shaped both the lens and us. We all see through slightly different lenses. We all see different worlds. What we think we see, we react to. And whether we are the victim or the warrior we believe ... *we are right!*

It doesn't have to be a trauma for this split to occur. It can be a simple environment that to a child continually *does not feel good*. There could be subtle levels of verbal abuse and criticism, which can echo back into that soul's story of persecution. The boy who is bullied by his father feels powerless; he bullies someone else to gain his power back. His anger drives him. Beneath his anger his fear of powerlessness owns him. Here is the birth of the perpetrator, the victimizer. Born from the experience of powerlessness and not feeling loved, the willfulness to control someone else is created.

But if the suppression of rage and terror and the need to control are the rigid and frozen keystones of their characters, then the true enduring *keystones of compassion* will be lacking. This lack of self-compassion has broken the Circle of giving and receiving. Self-compassion must first be given to the one who has endured the story. These could be traumatic stories of rape, childhood sexual abuse, the violence of war, or the subtler traumatic stories of abandonment, neglect, abuse, criticism, and so forth. It doesn't matter. In the effort to survive and be happy, a unified experience is divided in order to control emotional and even physical pain.

A *Moment* Is A Unified Experience

In the beginning, terror and rage are one unified movement. In any moment when we disconnect from what is happening, such as smiling when we are angry, the separation from the immediate emotional movement occurs. When there is a trauma this movement is paralyzed. We are unable to emotionally and physically run or fight. In this *moment* we are like any other animal attempting to survive. And like many animals we play dead, so to speak. We become numb to the feelings of the *moment*. As emotional beings, this survival can mean the deadening of emotions as well. In order to deaden to the trauma of this moment or event, the unified moment that is

Medicine of One

a complexity of terror and rage is split. In this split the emotional energies are paralyzed and separated so there is no terror in the rage and no rage in the terror.

There is a split in the great charges of emotional energy that were part of one *moment. Moment* means a unified experience. *This moment* could be hours long. This *unified moment* is divided and cemented into the wall of your protection. Split and polarized into the warrior, the anger is cold and can't access the true hurt of the warm bleeding heart. Cold, hard, and detached from the world of emotion, these people become inaccessible and unreachable. Tears can be a distant unknown experience to them. These warriors are revered and respected for their service to the abused and victimized, but they are cut off from themselves and the *grace of the flow,* and they cannot truly receive.

All movement occurs when opposites engage in a flow, like a battery with negative and positive poles. Even the earth itself has a magnetic power from the South and North Poles. The Hopi speak of these as the Twin Heroes who keep the earth in balance through their command of two serpents entwined around the axis of the earth from the North to the South poles. They are *two* coiled in a *flow* that creates the balance of *one*. Separated and unaligned with the intent of the Twin Heroes of keeping the earth as one harmonious web of life they could war with one another and cause there to be a world out of balance. The earth is a circle and the axis is its spine. The Twin Heroes serve the spine of the earth and bring the primal serpents into this service as well.

So these opposites originally emerge from the *flow* and reflect it. In this state they are unified, just as giving and receiving as the Circle of One are never separate. They, too, are part of a unified moment. But in both immediate and traumatic moments that threaten our survival, and in long term exposure to hurt and pain, this harmony and balance of opposites split.

Geronimo was a great warrior. Great warriors are revered and remembered. You could say that the warrior was one force or movement in his Circle. This warrior may have been in balance at one time until something tragic happened to

The Warrior and the Victim

his family and his people, and a story was born. In this story his warrior became fueled by rage. Who wouldn't consider his rage justifiable? If you witnessed the slaughter of your people and your family, the loss and the agony would be overwhelming. It could leave you immobilized without the will to live. Or your will could explode as a great war cry shattering the quiet of the dead and dying and you could snap into the opposite of this immobilization and *become* a Geronimo. Now, your grieving is perpetuated through an unquenchable vengeance. You live a life of running, hiding, and attacking.

You stand up to the perpetrators. You fight back. You kill them to ease your pain. You are mobilized ... mobilized by rage. Revenge and retribution become your purpose in life. Now the *righteous one* has been born. Trapped in a story, you raise your rifle to the sky as if for an eternity, life after life after life. There will be no peace, but you will protect the weak and you will fight for justice and be respected. You give endlessly to all and you will receive their material gifts of horses, food, and blankets. But will you weep on anyone's shoulder and receive their *love*?

This is an extreme story. But those who are in your *camp* will not perceive you as being reckless or vengeful. They will see power and strength. They will respect you, and so you are rewarded. But your rage is cut off and separated from its agony. You become owned by your agony as you go on seeing one injustice after another that you must fight, like one wall after another in the maze ... eternally. You are terrified of the opposite place ~ the powerless and the helpless. Never will you let this energy enter you.

This *you* that is the warrior is a spin in the Circle of the true you. It has usurped *all* of your identity unto itself. It's an identity grounded in your own internal self-perception and in how you are *perceived by others*. You, as this warrior, now function from the need to feel that power is in your control. Powerlessness and helplessness terrify you even in your apparent fearlessness. When witnessing or experiencing a story of abuse, cruelty, or injustice, you perceive it through the historical lens of your own soul story. This drives you to defend, protect, and control in situations that don't necessarily require a fight. You are driven by this time capsule of helplessness. You are always there to help another, but you are incapable of asking for help or receiving, because this true receiving would require engaging, an opening of your heart to the vulnerable small fragile feelings within. In your mind this would be like surrendering to weakness. The inability to have this kind of compassion toward yourself renders you incapable of receiving and incapable of uttering the words "help me" not only to another, but also incapable of even allowing these words to surface in your own mind.

You will have difficulty connecting to the softer, feminine side of feeling, intuition, and trust. You will only trust your own mind and intellect. Life will prove you are right as you see through the lens of your *old story*. You will think a lot. You will second-guess what people are thinking, what's down the road. You will appear strong and confident, but when you sleep the terror comes, unable to be contained in the mental prison. When there is no war to fight you will be empty and depressed.

Your rage should have exploded like a stick of flaming dynamite, a fire fueled by the pain and the grief of your loss touched by the tremendous helplessness over not being able to restore what has been lost. The victim and warrior in this moment of expression should have been unified. But instead, to balance the scales of justice, the rage becomes cold and calculating. It is as if the rage, having been set fire in the very pelvis and bowels of its origin, climbs up into the analytical and detached mind. Your anger is cold because it's separated from the pain, from the hurt, from the powerlessness. You are protected, but hard. You are honorable, but inaccessible. In this inaccessibility you can give, but you cannot truly receive.

Again and again people with great achievement and success come to me. They are generous and compassionate toward others and their tough, hard warriors have given them the strength to do great things. Yet they come to me because they do not have peace. They come to me because the warrior runs their Circle rather than serving it. They come to me because they can give, but they cannot trust and receive. These people can be great leaders and heroes on the battlefields of

The Warrior and the Victim

politics, human rights, natural catastrophes, and war.

The best soldiers are emotionally detached. They will do anything for others and are protectors. They have a great sense of honor and high standards of behavior. They are not perpetrators, but they are cut off from the delicate feelings of the victim, from themselves, and from intimacy with themselves and others. This being *cut off* is reflected in the inability to trust and receive. They have cut the thread to the true self through their refusal of compassion for their hungry ghost and are trapped in the maze of isolation.

Imagine a sculpture of the warrior in which the artist is portraying someone who can give everything, but whose heart is closed to receiving. In addition to the posture of the body, the artist is using the hands to speak *sign language* to express the psychological dichotomy. This is called a *psychological gesture,* a kind of inner stance. The warrior sends two messages at the same time. His giving hand is outstretched strongly and is firmly open as he stands straight and tall with a giving, even gentle smile. But his other hand is held out like a traffic officer stopping traffic. *Don't come any closer.* This stance leads to isolation. In isolation, the blockage of receiving does not allow for replenishment. Rain falls from the sky, but this stance is like dry hard packed earth that can't absorb the water. It just rinses over it and doesn't sink into the ground and replenish the reservoirs. One day the well may run dry with depression and desperation, because nothing can flow back in. Now he is the *victim* of his own warrior.

The list is endless of great warriors throughout history who died for others. Often these great warriors have an *old soul story* in them where they led their people forward and gave everything to protect them. But the odds were against them and they were unable to save those they loved. Even though they may have sacrificed their lives, in the moment of their death as they look around at the dead and dying, the great weight of failure is their last memory and belief.

Even if it's a story from childhood the same feeling of failure can still haunt them, so they keep trying to win the war over and over again. Even if the story is one of victory it's the same old groove. They still keep trying to win. They perceive a war where there isn't one and feel they must keep on fighting.

This is not a description of everyone who fights back, stands up to injustice, or fights for justice. Gandhi stood up for justice. Nelson Mandela fought for justice. Chief Joseph declared, "I will fight no more, forever." These are people whose agony did not own them. Somehow, they found the path to their own peace. Somehow, even in their *warriorship*, they walked the path of compassion for all ~ even for the perpetrator. They stood in the center of the Circle of giving and receiving. They anchored themselves in the truth of who they were and brought justice into the world peacefully. But these are the *Christs*. These are the *awakened ones*.

The opposite side of this warrior *coin of great tragedy* is immobilization, shutting down, depression, and the loss of the will to live. Lightning strikes and you cannot move. You cannot breathe. It's as if life has suddenly rushed out of you as the dead and the dying lay all around you. It's as if you have been electrocuted by a tragedy that is simply too much for your nervous system. You are suddenly hurled into the land of limbo and the lost. The mouth of the soul opens but no sound escapes. If the threat is great and offers no exit, then the only route of escape is to jettison yourself out into the spirit world where it seems you cannot be touched ... where it seems you are safe. But now you have left behind *the one* who suffered the experience, trapped in the dark cave where it fled, buried alive by your own *survivalist mind*. There was no other way to survive.

This is a shut down and a kind of paralysis. *Lost* and *soul loss* are words that touch this place. You lose your will to live and do not want to be here in this world. You sink into the powerless and the helpless.

The polarized victim can't access the warrior. They swim in their victimhood, in their tears. They live in constant powerlessness and helplessness. They can cry at the drop of a hat. This victimhood is a survival tactic as well. Rather than the outward moving force of the warrior that protects with a hard boundary, theirs is a shrinking energy that wants to draw us into their story. The victim gives and their receiving is like that of a sponge. They hunger for a particular kind of attention

The Warrior and the Victim

and know how to magnetize other people's energy toward themselves through their behavior. Unlike the warrior who has a hard boundary, the victim has little or no boundaries. As a result, victims can energetically take on the emotional weight of others. This is usually because somewhere inside they are in resonance with the other person's story. Two people who are polarized in their victim are like resonating tuning forks. One seems to rescue the other, but in so doing they add weight to their own inner victim's suffering. They see the helpless all around them. Rather than own that helplessness in themselves with compassion, the *victim* directs their compassion to the victims outside of themselves, being unable to give it to the victim within.

The victim's *psychological gesture* depicting the inner dichotomy like that of the warrior's, sends two messages: they are open to giving and they are closed to receiving. Their *inner stance* would be the outstretched hand as if reaching out to give, leaning forward and off balance as if wanting in the same moment. The other hand sign is a fist pressed against their heart, as if *signing* that the victim owns them in that clenched hand. It seems like they receive but they are actually feeding their *hungry ghost* and are taking.

It's natural to feel for people who are immersed in their victimhood. But if they are people we know, we can start to feel manipulated and controlled. Anchoring in the victim is as much a mode of control as is the warrior's. In this inhibition of movement and control of *emotion* we separate from our inner life and we separate from the greater life that we are part of.

We can find plenty of labels for our condition: isolation, disconnection, loneliness ... but not peace. So now we have labeled and judged ourselves. These become more split off movements in the Circle. They are spins that generate thinking as self-criticism. We believe this thinking and energize it. Our desperation grows. The strength of the labels grows. The hole we dig with our minds gets deeper. The dirt starts falling in and on and on it goes.

Rage drives the warrior. Terror drives the victim. The victim's energy falls in on itself as opposed to the warrior's, whose hard shield of protection is pushed out. The victim has no boundary. The warrior will protect and push forward those who can't protect themselves. Each sees themselves in those who suffer injustice; but the warrior and the victim have different energetic reactions. They can also be a combination of both. These are the extremes. Most of humanity will find themselves polarizing toward the victim, or the warrior; and in some cases, depending on the situation, they can flip between one or the other. Both the warrior and the victim hate the powerless feelings of the victim. Both believe their own stories. The warrior doesn't talk about it and the victim can't stop talking about it.

Harmony of Opposites

So is there an *old story* within you, which you keep living as either the victim or the warrior? If you are still here now, still alive in this very moment, whatever you did to survive, whatever force stepped in for your preservation, thank it. Thank it compassionately, but be strong in your earnestness to no longer let it rule the Circle of who you are from the dissociation of rage and terror. This can be either as the victim or the warrior. It's time for liberation and the union of opposites to flow together in service to the Circle of you.

The emotional polarities are uncountable and unnamable. But that which is moving in a moment of intensity is beyond a word that defines and labels an emotion. This is why we turn to metaphors and the poetics of language to talk about it. This is why there is healing through dance, drawing, writing, and any art form that translates our inner world into something more tangible.

Through this specific expression we are able to engage our inner life and let it speak, let it move. This is why the *Soul Dreaming* I do can be a very poetic and emotional journey and why the use of *Primordial Movements* draws on the wisdom of the body and the magic of sound. They transcend sterile definitions and allow one to reenter the *moment* too complex to define with the mind and yet, specific and *palpable*.

Opposites attract. Why is that? Why is it so often in relationships that a victim partners with a warrior? Perhaps it

The Warrior and the Victim

is this separated self-seeking *wholeness*. One will be needy and the other will need to be needed. The victim will have no protection, no boundary, and the warrior will provide the feeling of protection and safety. One will be vulnerable and full of emotion; the other will be stoic, always calm, but often impenetrable. The very thing that was attractive becomes a repelling force in each of them. The warrior's distance and unexpressiveness will provoke the needs of the victims. As these needs intensify, the warrior will need to withdraw from the feeling of being smothered. And unless they each become responsible for the feelings that move within them they will blame each other for being the cause. If they could each see the other as a reflection of what they have disowned in themselves, they could choose to participate in their relationship as a path of self-healing. If they could both choose to first cultivate self-compassion for the unloved within themselves, then that love could be the Circle to the other. This relationship is simply another way of discussing a relationship with ourselves.

These are the great enemies of control: tears, anger, rage, terror. These are at the dark core of the victim and the warrior. Our whole life is constructed around avoiding them. No matter how much rational understanding we have of ourselves this is the one place we are unlikely to enter on our own through our own efforts. We may think we have, but our minds are very clever.

Opposites create movement. From this movement, the world and everything come into being. The Medicine of One allows all opposites to move by being the love they move *in* and not listening to the righteous thinking. Balance comes from the integration of the disowned opposite. Connecting the opposites brings us back into the flow. When they merge, you can't control the deep feelings which come that can be a mixture of true anger and fear, and feelings of powerlessness and helplessness. If you can surrender to their merging, great movement and transformation comes.

The *way back home* to their *true self* is to make peace with the *fragile* within, the time capsule of helplessness and powerlessness. Any warrior who cannot allow the vibrations of the victim to move through them is terrified of their victim, the enemy within. Any victim who seems completely paralyzed by their fear and in constant anxiety is in a constant state of flight from their terror. This inaccessible terror prevents true trust and true receiving. They are seemingly different in the victim and the warrior but both involve a loving, honoring engagement of the fragile without getting involved in its thinking, its story. Both also bring back the fire.

The victim knows little about the warrior fire and the warrior knows little about the fire of the soft, loving passion of the victim. Each holds a key to the balancing of the other. Separated from one another, neither *fire* is balanced. Both must give up their stories at some point. Both must give up believing in the thinking that holds their story in place. Both must learn the *true action of self-love* to integrate the energy of their pain. *Harmony of the opposites* happens spontaneously when both are brought into the *Circle of compassion.*

Liberation and the Flow of Giving and Receiving

Life in balance gives and receives as an unbroken cycle. There is no true giving without receiving, and there is no true receiving without giving. To truly receive is to be in the flow of giving and receiving when your giving becomes a giving of yourself. Giving yourself immediately invokes receiving just as in the flow of true communication. When listening and speaking are a balanced reciprocal flow there is giving and receiving.

In this *sign language* of the human body the gesture of unity of giving and receiving is both hands outstretched, hand and fingers open to the sky as if catching the rain from above and fingers radiating forward with life giving energy to the world or a person. The Circle is unbroken. The arms are widely spaced to freely give of the *heart filled self.* There is no reaching forward off-balance with need. The person that gives and receives *stands* like a tree rooted in the earth receiving nutrients and water and giving this moisture back to the air, and its leaves return to the earth in fall bringing nutrients and new life to the ground. True receiving and true giving are not

The Warrior and the Victim

divided. They cannot be separated.

This immediate present, this moment in which you are here reading these words, is where the experience of *One* is. It's the doorway to the truth of who you are. This moment is always here. The question is ... *where are you?* And where were you in the most difficult moments or events in your life? Surviving can often mean separating from the moment, from the ongoing present. These lost rejected *moments* separate you from the immediate moment of right now as immobilized emotion and as incessant survival thinking. The Medicine of One is about dissolving the separation, bringing split off moments back into one *eternal moment*.

If who you are is expressed as a presence like the spacious, quiet Circle, if this deep listening presence swimming motionless in the flow is who you are, if its manifestation in this world is the spine of your life ... then true giving of yourself must be giving of this presence. The *spine of your life*, regardless of uniqueness, is this channeling of reception and giving. Whatever you give you receive first. Your true self is ever receptive and ever giving in its presence. When you anchor yourself in it you are the unity of giving and receiving.

When you lovingly give your compassion to what moves inside of you, what was imprisoned is freed and gifts you with your own energy. Your compassionate attention as the Circle allows the flow. Giving and receiving is the flow of a relationship with self, with the world, and with others.

When I am with someone in the Circle helping them and they earnestly commit, we stand in the flow of giving and receiving. I listen to their wisdom and awareness and let it guide me to guide them. They receive the guidance meant to open them up to receive from within. Listening opens us up to receiving, and listening to another is giving. So listening is a perfect example of this indivisible flow.

I always try to share from my life. I never ask anyone to do something I won't do. I may invoke an emotional energy for them and in its moving through me they see, feel, and receive it. In their receiving something moves inside of them that gives to themselves, to the Circle and to me. It all happens in an instant. And we laugh a lot. And we cry. We laugh uncontrollably together in a way that each infects the other. Who is giving and who is receiving? Together we love the warrior and the victim and free them so they can bring their gifts to the Circle.

Challenge yourself to be the Circle to the victim and the warrior and receive by exposing yourself in those times of great difficulty. Touch the fragile inside of yourself. Let your whimpering tremble through you and dare to let another see it, to share this trembling moment. Stand in the center as the big I joining heaven and earth with arms outstretched to receive and to give.

Chapter Fourteen

Peace: How We Meet Our Losses
*The absolute truth of you can
never be lost, only forgotten.*

Loss is a story we all know. You cannot live in this world and escape the experience of loss. Our world changes throughout our life; loss is almost always a component of this change that encourages growth and transformation. Change, evolution, new worlds, new universes, and new life emerge from the flow between chaos and order.

As a very young man I explored the ideas of science and philosophy. I was looking for the key of our existence, evolution, and movement. I had a big black binder I used to record my discoveries. One of these discoveries was the awareness of this flow between chaos and order. I knew this principle I discovered wasn't unique. I was just sorting things out for myself that ancient peoples had discovered long ago. You can call it chaos and order, dark and light, yin and yang, Apollo and Dionysus, Shakti and Shiva. It doesn't matter. Within this constant flux and change on the human level is the experience of loss.

Loss is about losing a relationship. Our personal world is like no one else's world. Our specific relationships to people, animals, our health and well being experienced as *our body*, are different for all of us. The impact of these losses will not be the same from one person to another. For many animal owners, their pets are their children that they care for and love. When a pet dies one of their children has died. Of course,

Medicine of One

they know animals don't have the longevity of humans. This knowledge is always there in the background. But it doesn't make the loss any easier. Even losing our relationships to objects like our houses, cars, and possessions, which are important and meaningful in our lives can be very traumatic.

I am reminded of Tom Hank's character in the movie *Cast Away*. His plane crashes somewhere in the ocean and he is the lone survivor. He struggles for years to survive on an island alone, catching fish, eating fruit, and sleeping in a cave. He finds a volleyball manufactured by Wilson Sporting Goods. It has *Wilson* written on it. He paints a face on it and that volleyball with a face becomes his companion and friend, *Wilson*. It is his most important relationship. Eventually he builds a raft and sets out on the ocean with Wilson to find his way back home. One day he falls asleep as the waters flood over the raft rinsing Wilson into the waves. He struggles to get "him" back, but he can't. He loses Wilson, his best friend, to the infinite ocean and cries in agony. Now he is truly alone and lost on a raft in the ocean, riding a current to he knows not where ~ because he lost a volleyball? No, because he lost the most meaningful – *in the moment* – relationship in his life.

When you lose something big, you lose the world you know, that you have come to feel comfortable in, and which, inevitably, you identify with. So the loss will shake your whole world ... all of your habits. If you try to force things to stay the same or hang on to the old path, you will find a kind of deadness in them. They won't give you what they did and you can sink into a feeling of being *lost*. *Loss* can easily lead to the feeling of *lost*.

You have to give up the old meaning for new meaning to come. So meaningfulness is not something fixed. Give up the idea and the belief that it should be meaningful. Just because that which seemed meaningful to you before no longer does is no reason to adopt the belief that your life is meaningless now. You may have to live in the void, in the still quiet of nothing, in the place from which all creation stirs. Let it be okay and do not believe in the thinking born from this pain of the *empty*. It is not the truth. It's just your mind clawing at the walls of the *dark nothing* while it's trying to climb out of the

Peace: How We Meet Our Losses

void on the backs of the dead. And all the while, the dead weight of unmoved grief keeps pulling you down.

You might say to me, "What do you mean 'unmoved?' I've been crying every day for three years?" But what thoughts are attached to those tears and thoughts you keep believing? And what is gone that you refuse to let slide out of your grieving grip? You can't hang onto your loss anymore than you can hang onto the wind. Who am I, if there is nothing to hang onto so that I can say, "This is my life, this is me"? How can we be with the vacancy, the emptiness? Where will the meaning come from?

So many tears and sadness, but what of your irrational anger and rage? I am not saying irrational to mean unjustified. None of the movements in the Circle need to be justified. Much of the problem comes from your reliance on your rational, analytical mind. Believe me. Many psychiatrists and psychologists come to me for help. Why, since they have such a perfect *rational* understanding of the source of their feelings? It is the feelings that don't fit into the *self-image* you hold of yourself that are always the problem ... the ones you can't imagine and can't fathom within yourself. The stories of loss can have many movements. And they all must move. So you must allow all possibilities, even the unimaginable.

My dogs are my greatest teachers. They are my children, my friends and companions, and my helpers. It is rare that they are not by my side. We share a home and roam the land together. They teach me about caring for and loving them regardless of how I may be feeling myself. They are frequently a very important presence for the people who visit me for help. They teach me about presence and alertness. But they also teach me about the consequences of carelessness and recklessness. They are wild and instinctual and they get to live out this side of their nature because of the life we share. But this means they live in a far more dangerous world than *backyard dogs*. They suffer injuries chasing deer, rabbits, javelinas, and skunks. The skunks are most often what they catch. These injuries lead to shorter lives when they can't walk anymore. The potential for accidental death is always present. Dogs and wolves do not live nearly as long as we do, even when they die of old age. In the last 25 years five of my dogs have returned to being wolf spirits again.

I have a special wall in my house with the pictures of the wolf-bear dogs who have graced my life and are now gone. Every one of these dogs has taught me in manifold ways about myself, about working with emotions, about dogs and their world. Had I not loved and cared for them I would not have experienced any of these losses. But then I would know nothing about life. They taught me to let go of my need for them, and not to hold on to them so tightly that I prevent their spirits from experiencing the full spectrum of their soul. And they taught me to go on loving, despite the certainty that I will lose what I love, and that emptiness will visit me along with a host of feelings depending on the unique story of that loss.

My experiences with the dogs mirror many stories that happen in our lives as humans. These stories echo through *soul time* setting into motion the ancient, as well as the present, emotions. So my presence with their loss is a healing that transcends time. Without their unique living presence and their deaths there would be no Medicine of One. They have graced and gifted me with a wisdom born from experience. Experiences that sometimes brought very difficult outcomes because of my choices and mistakes.

Three and half years ago I was on my way to a Circle to work with Jane who was on a *Vision Quest* and had spent the entire night alone in the Circle. It was May and the air was cooler than normal for that time of year, in the 70's rather than close to 100 degrees. My two dogs Cheyenne and Hanta Yo were accompanying me, each in their own unique way, Cheyenne leading the way and Hanta Yo trailing behind. I was both present with our walk to the Circle and with Jane who was awaiting our arrival. Twenty-five yards ahead of me I heard Cheyenne make a very odd growl, like something had annoyed her. It was not a sound I had heard her make in the wild before so I was alerted to the path ahead. Something was off and I had a feeling what it was. This was perfect weather for rattlesnakes to be on the move. When it's cold they hibernate, when it's too hot they stay in the shade. I rushed up ahead and there was a very large Mojave Green Rattlesnake snaking across our

Peace: How We Meet Our Losses

trail. I went back, leashed Hanta Yo, guided him clear of the snake, and ran to Cheyenne who was cresting the top of the mesa. I inspected her and saw the two bleeding spots on her front right leg. She had been nipped before and had healed from the poison, as had another one of my dog friends, Osha, after having been bitten in the face. I was upset, but not panicked. I took her back to the truck so she would not move around excessively and went to the Circle to finish up with Jane.

When I returned to the truck Cheyenne seemed to be doing well. I went straight to the veterinarian. Neither one of us felt drastic action was necessary like antivenom medicine. I began antibiotics right away, as well as massive doses of Echinacea, an old folk remedy that had worked well with Osha. Each day her strength faded and her leg swelled more. I called the vet after the weekend. She said to make sure she got plenty of fluids. Worry was in my Circle. I neither rejected it with over confidence, nor fueled it to panic with obsessive thoughts. That evening I had to carry her into the house. She couldn't walk. I laid her down in her favorite spot, gave her an antibiotic pill, held her for a while, kissed her on the cheek, and went to bed.

I got up the next morning and jumped out of bed to see how she was doing. I entered the room where she had been resting the night before. I could see her body was without the movement of breathing ... she was gone. It was imperative that I breathed and kept breathing through all the movements of *my* journey with her death.

The first feeling to be honored was when I called a friend to tell them I could not meet with them on that day. I hesitated to say why. I did not want to say the words ... but I did, "Cheyenne is dead." When I got off the phone I leaped into my agonizing rage without questioning it and screamed over and over, "I don't wanna say it! I don't wanna say it! I don't wanna say it!"

In writing this section I was hesitant to involve you in the whole story because it was not my intent to sadden you. But whatever you feel, and even feeling *nothing* is something, honor it as your own, as if somehow this story is resonating

Medicine of One

with one of your own in memory or in the ancient history of your soul. Let it be about *you* and that which knows the feeling of loss within *you*. Don't feel for me. Feel for yourself. Own it within *you*. This is the gift of these stories when we read them or see them in cinema. If you do this something within you is honored and moves. If you put it outside yourself as *my* story it will keep cycling back and remain as an unmoved burden of grief. If you feel a soft sadness of empathy and it easily lifts, just let that be. Allow and be with whatever you feel. Don't bring your mind into it. This story serves several purposes as an illustration of loss and, perhaps, as an experience of loss.

When I buried Cheyenne in the deep hole I had dug in the back of my house I found one large rock at the bottom, a heart. So from this dream of death the gravedigger unearthed a heart from the ground of transformation. I could feel the stubbornness inside of me struggle as I lay her stiff body in the bottom of the grave. I did not want to perform this action. I did not!

As I lowered her gently into the soft cool hand of the earth, I began to sing a song I wrote for my first wolf dog, Dakota, who died of cancer.

> *Here I lay through the night*
> *'Til the bright dawning light*
> *Waiting around 'til you find me*
> *Oh you look out the door*
> *I'm not breathin' any more*
> *But don't worry that's not really me*
>
> *I am what I am*
> *A wolf spirit again*
> *And I'll be with you always my friend.*
> *In our life I was free*
> *You just let me be*
> *Wild, wooly, and true*
>
> *Now it's all up to you*
> *To be wild and true*

Peace: How We Meet Our Losses

Be the man of your dreams
Be the soul that you are
I'm the fire in your eyes
Now it's all up to you
To be wild and true

Oh you carried me down
To the river's flowing sound
And you placed me beneath the willow trees
In the softness of sand
You laid me in God's Hands
Then you listened to the sound of the breeze
I am what I am
A wolf spirit again
And I'll be with you always my friend
In our life I was free
You just let me be
Wild, wooly, and true

Now it's all up to you
To be wild and true
Be the man of your dreams
Be the soul that your are
I'm the fire in your eyes
Now it's all up to you to be wild and true
It's all up to you to be wild and true

  The most difficult moment was laying the first shovel full of dirt. I yelled "I can't, I can't throw the dirt on her. I don't believe it." With each shovel full my body was racked with tears, until a kind of fury filled the hole with dirt.
  On the unearthed heart rock I wrote *Cheyenne* and placed it on a pedestal over the grave. I did not bury my heart with her. I demanded of myself to stay present to every movement. It was a complicated web of rights and wrongs. Though not absolute, it was likely that some of my own actions had carried her into the arms of death despite the initial lash of a rattlesnake's bite. To let the memories and emotions flood through me as they wished, while being the loving Circle to

that part of me that wanted to hang on to the memories of my beautiful friend was a challenge.

Cheyenne's death was also the death of some of my way of life. When the wind blew I could see and feel her. It was her physical absence that prevailed in the beginning of my mourning. The places I would go and sit for hours with my other dog, Hanta Yo, felt emptier without her presence. Hanta was already getting more stubborn and seemed to age suddenly right before Cheyenne's death. With her death he became even slower. Would I lose him soon, too? Was this world we shared about to completely disappear? Of course the places weren't going anywhere, but so much of the meaning in our present lives gets caught up and anchored in memories. Cheyenne's presence with me in these places could not be separated from my experience of them. Avoiding them would be avoiding my feelings of loss, two of which are the *empty* and the *nothing*.

The meaningfulness of how we experience the world is not something that is unchanging. Remember, it is the nature of life and this world to change. It is important to surrender into the *empty*, into the feeling of meaningless so you can reemerge into a world of new meaning. This may feel like an anchor tugging at us while we drift on a sea of uncertainty. Wondering whether we will drown in the *nothing* and not come back may be a fear. I felt the fear without believing in the thought, without getting swept along in it.

For several weeks I could feel *I don't believe it* lurking in the Circle. I know my heart will soar when that tight *I don't believe it* breathes out and I surrender it all, allowing the empty space to fill. For in hanging on tightly to life we fortify the emptiness as our constant companion.

When you lose what you love, be with your loss in all its forms and movements, but don't get entangled in thoughts born in the separateness. Some will be righteous and some will be full of self-blame. Be willing to let the wind of purification sweep away every thread of clinging memory. Does this mean you don't get to remember? Of course not ... but don't hang on. Let the memories visit you like a leaf falling from a tree.

Peace: How We Meet Our Losses

Loss comes in many forms and will spare no one. You can try and spare yourself from the pain by moving away from it, by trapping it in various forms of thinking, but then this becomes the true loss, the loss of Self. Too many losses handled this way will leave you safe from the pain of loss but dead to life. To stay in life you have to go through the doorways of these deaths as the spacious Medicine of One to every spin in the Circle. This spaciousness, this quiet presence, roots you into what will never die and is without definition, memory, or personality. That which was there before you were born, and will be there when your physical body expires, is the absolute truth of *You* and is the one thing you cannot lose. But if you harden to life's losses it will seem as if you have lost your deepest Self. Death's doorway will stand in the way, blocked by your own stubbornness. You can't pretend the stubbornness isn't there. It is important to neither deny the tight fist of control, nor let it *own you* and *run your Circle,* so to speak. Commit to being your vast, loving, spaciously breathing *Self of the Circle* to that tight fist, allowing it to clench the flower bud of trapped energy until it can implode no more and must now reverse motion and explode as flowering feelings and surrender.

The way out of the *dark nothing* into new meaning comes from bringing the unmoved and unloved into the Circle of One that you are. These movements will spin forth from the story around your loss. This loss is usually a relationship to things, people, animals, objects, places, your body, your health, your job ... anything that is experienced. Walking away from your pain is a rejection that traps something precious in yourself. A *beauty within you* becomes entombed and forgotten.

You might ask, "How can you say that? What is the beauty in being rejected by someone you love? What is it I am gaining? I don't see it! I feel worthless! Hopelessly lost. I will be alone."

In our effort to avoid the pain of loss we try to avoid what reminds us of our loss. What perhaps we once loved and enjoyed in life we now stay clear of. This is true with anything, not just loss ~ anything which challenges us to feel what we stubbornly don't want to feel in order to sustain the illusion of control and safety. So from the fortress we have fashioned out of bricks made of trapped pain, we keep life out and then the garden of our heart withers and dies. The labyrinth of life that should carry us through life like the opening of a flower protectively closes in and traps us in a maze of false safety.

We are in absolute control, stuck in the core of our self-made prisons. We become trapped in the very mechanisms we set in place to protect ourselves from pain. And so the avoidance of pain is like dumbly delivering our life and our freedom to the *guardian of the heart.* This guardian is strong, opinionated, resolute, and willful. But it functions from fear, not the love of all that you are. It prevents you from being who you are. It polarizes your Circle into its small, separated, hard, defensive little **i**-*ness* and it rules the Circle of who you are by posing as your strength when, in fact, it is a strength out of balance that undermines your true feeling of strength, a strength married to trust and comfortable with surrender.

Again and again, you will encounter a movement, a force, and a spin in your Circle that would have you mistake it for your *self*. Blindly, we live our lives wandering through the maze, with survival as our main concern and the so-called protector/controller as our guide. We have forgotten how to listen to the deeper whispers of guidance, which are as subtle as the movements of a compass needle.

The presence of the Medicine of One in every moment of my life has freed me to love, to live, and to have clarity about who I am. No matter what difficulty you have faced or is before you now, and no matter what your loss ... how you meet it and how you engage it moment by moment will determine whether your future is full of suffering. It will determine if you are free and can live in peace.

It's the presence you bring to each moment that counts, not your analysis of that moment. You can cultivate all this vast knowledge of the human world, but how long can you remain quiet and be the stillness that you are? How long can you be free of thinking? This is the measure of your wisdom. And this quiet, *no thinking spaciousness* is the *Circle of the Medicine of One.*

Part Three

THE GREAT MYSTERY

Medicine of One

When he looked at the clouds coming toward him he saw the Kachina spirits bringing the fertility of rain. When he looked at the clouds he saw all the ancestors watching over the people and it made him smile. He didn't need to believe it was truth in order to feel safe in the world. He just allowed the gift of the clouds to have many forms and magic. He knew it was his own mind he saw, for he always stood beyond it as the pure blue sky to all things. He thought, this is who I am but why not enjoy all this wondrous beauty? When you live in the center of the Circle in which all things move, all things get to be real, born from the one.

From The Circle of Life
Lomakayu

Chapter Fifteen

I Don't Know

*Everything you think you are and everything
you think you know moves in the Circle of truth that you are,
invoked by the sacred words "I don't know."*

I don't know.

Three simple words that can be uttered in moments of little consequence and in moments of great tragedy. Three simple words that can invoke the suffering of helplessness or the great wisdom of truth. The first could be invoked by a question to a doctor, *am I going to die?* And the second invoked by the question *who am I?* For it was Plato's Socrates that spoke, "The only true wisdom is in knowing you know nothing."

My good friend Amy took her life. She told me she was tired so she was *checking out.* I did everything I could think of to stop her. Regardless, she was determined and followed through. Yes, she was having money problems and was facing a possible illness, and her beautiful dog friend Chasta was aging and seemed to be near the end of her life. But when someone asked me ... "Why did she do it"? The truth was I really didn't know. I could understand her character as the war between the Warrior and the Victim. I could *believe* that my reasoning was the truth. And perhaps this belief would give me the false security of knowing *why* and a shaky peace from that illusory understanding. My so-called *knowing* would just be my opinion. I would then believe that opinion and, perhaps when discussing it with someone, hold fast to my point of view

Medicine of One

as the truth. I would then believe I was right.

This *I don't know* is invoked by the deep profound questions we encounter in our journey through life: Why do I have cancer? Who will take care of me now that I am alone and aging? Will I be alone for the rest of my life? We often desperately want to know the answer. We believe we need to have the answer in order to have peace.

Recently, a jet liner disappeared with over two hundred people on board. Thousands of miles of ocean have been searched looking for a sign of debris. A *ping* was detected from the black box and searchers began to scan the ocean bottom. Relatives of the missing were sobbing and crying as they waited for news and grew furious with the airline company's ineptness. To this day the jet liner has not been found. The majority of relatives and friends remain in their misery needing to *know*. What if the truth is never known? Will the tight grip of this *need to know* go on for their whole lives?

One of my wolf dogs literally went missing one day. He came to me through the Jerome Humane Society. They knew I had just lost one of my dogs and thought I could help a stray someone had found roaming the streets. He was gray, black and white, and had the face of a bear. In the world of totems the bear is connected to healing and healers. Bear is the earth element as he lumbers on all fours contrasted to the Eagle that soars in the skies seeing great distances.

I named him Osha, which is the name of a powerful healing plant used by the Northwest Indians. It is also known as *Bear Medicine* because bears were known to roll around it its roots when they felt ill. Osha was true to his name, as his teddy bear presence and ease with people helped them relax. Like all my wolf dogs he would lay next to them when I was doing a *Soul Dreaming*. He was that *bear grounding force* for them.

I had to leave Osha and Cheyenne with a friend at my house, while I left on a five-day trip with a client to the Four Corners. I returned in the afternoon of the fifth day. Apparently their caretaker had allowed them to be loose outside with the front door open. They had run off after something several hours before. A neighbor called to tell me Cheyenne was over

I Don't Know

by her home. I picked her up and then began my search for Osha.

I searched for six weeks and ran ads in the paper. I had to find him. I needed to know he was okay. Did someone take him? Was he dead? Was he still wandering around out there? There was no answer but it was important to live out my need to search for him for as long as necessary. This was part of my journey of healing. From the beginning, I had to bring my worry, my sadness, my desperation, my need to search and search, my need to *know* into the Circle. This meant that I kept breathing, relaxing, and surrendering. It meant that in honoring my need to search, the desperation did not need to own me and drive me endlessly. It meant that at some point without any evidence as to what happened, I had to live with the truth of *I don't know*. Throughout this whole journey being the Circle to it all meant not getting involved in my thinking, but doing what I had to do. It was a balance between honoring my feelings and needs, yet rooting myself in the greater Circle of who I am ... a presence, which is a compassionate quiet awareness.

After six weeks of chasing one false lead after another, the spin of feelings I continued to bring into the Circle began to settle. Without deciding anything, the willingness to live with my loss as something lingering in the unknown was something I could now surrender to.

I never found Osha.

Everyday, children disappear as victims of kidnapping or killing. Their parents don't know if their children are dead or alive. They don't know where they are. They don't know if they will ever see them again. Daily, hourly, it's always on their mind. No matter what happened, they need to know. They must know.

You can imagine the many possibilities of what happened. Years and years can pass by and you can hang onto the belief you will find them and one day they will come home to you. If you desperately hang onto this idea, rather than just letting it be one of the many possibilities, then the story never ends and owns you ... perhaps forever. In addition to the possibilities of what happened are all the possibilities of *if only I had done something differently.* These all invoke *thinking* and *believing.*

It takes a rare connection to the deep self to let the *I don't know* prevail and yet, to let all the possibilities be there in the Circle without trying to hang onto those that give you comfort. By hanging onto the comforting imaginings you also keep the less desirable imaginings lingering beneath it. In hanging on, the mind will never stop energizing your thoughts and you will suffer. You will also find ways to blame yourself adding cement to the stones of your unmoved pain. The thinking mind from which there is no exit will become your personal hell of suffering, unless this hell is brought into the Circle and you align with that Circle as the truth of who you are. If you continue to live this truth as a path of life the pain and suffering of the story will fade as all the feelings move in the Circle that is free of beliefs. Suffering is born from aligning and abiding in what you are not. You are not what you think or what you believe.

Giving up believing in our thinking and giving up being right is a great challenge for most of us. It is the willingness to invoke *I don't know.* How many times each day do we respond to what is happening based on what we think we know? If we could all have a little more *I don't know* in our lives there would be more peace in the world. Countries go to war based on what they think they know. The most recent instance of this was the war in Iraq where it was taken as truth that they had *weapons of mass destruction.* This turned out to be false.

I have shared many of my own stories in this book and within almost every one of them is this *I don't know.* After 40 years of physical and neurological difficulties from my accident, I still continue my search for balance through my daily routines. When the thought stirs, *what's the point,* I just become the Circle to its hopelessness without believing it. Will I have to live with this difficulty as it is now for the rest of my life? *I don't know.* The underlying feeling of this *I don't know* is not a hopeless answer to the question. It's an - *I don't know* - which is actually filled with a peaceful surrender. It's an - *I don't know* - which invokes the Circle of the Medicine of One.

Many of us pursue careers that satisfy us. We learn

I Don't Know

skills. The spine of our life channels through this work and we feel good about that. But then maybe something stirs within us wanting expression. What seemed to be our calling starts to become an effort. The stirring may first appear as a loss of interest in what you are currently doing, the way you are doing it, or even as feeling tired and frustrated with it all. Things bother you that didn't bother you before. The same thing can happen with a relationship or marriage. With the thought of change comes the thought, *what will I do if I don't do this?* If it's our work we *don't know* what it will look like. If we just stop, how will we survive, pay the bills, etc.? If it's a relationship the same questions of financial security and the idea of *being alone* can cause us to be deaf to the sounds of change within us. We need to know what the future looks like in order to meet the present. The space between the present and the future is filled with *I don't know* and it can paralyze us with the fear. To surrender to *I don't know* and move forward, the fear must be brought into the Circle and allowed to shimmer through you. Through this shimmering comes the trust in *I don't know.*

When this book goes out into the world it could echo back to me in ways that *I don't know.* Changes that stir within me now could be given form. But the present is this very moment of putting these words down. In this present, I trust. In this *I don't know* ~ I live.

And then there is the great question of self-inquiry, *who am I?* After you have crossed off every possible answer on the list and arrive at *I don't know,* now you just sit in the experience of that. That experience is thoughtless. What can be *thought* when you truly surrender to *I don't know?* If you take a deep breath and sigh *I don't know* to the ground and stay there, you become the quiet peaceful Circle of your true presence. Through *I don't know,* you become the answer to *who am I.* To touch it you have to become thoughtless. It's empty. It doesn't hold onto anything. It's like an open hand feeling the breeze.

These three simple words are a sacred invocation if you embody them. So learn how to embody these words. Be *I don't know* to all your *needing to know* no matter what it is. Search, honor your feelings, but be the, *I don't know sacred Cir-*

Medicine of One

cle of you to it all. Everything you think you are and everything you think you know moves in the Circle of truth that you are, invoked by the sacred words *I don't know*. Hold your hands in prayer to your chest and bow, uttering, "I don't know, I don't know," and in that bowing join *The Great Mystery*.

Chapter Sixteen

Surrender

*Surrender is a gradual path that uses your loving
awareness, without judgment, in relationship to all that
moves within you. Surrender is married to compassion.
They both melt to the ground from the center and expand
spaciously as the Circle with your very breath.*

What does it mean to surrender? What does it mean to *you* to surrender? The first is a general question and the second is very specific to *you*. Probe all the possibilities of the first question. Now explore the answers to the second question. More than likely when you answer the second question the answers will be almost identical to the first. The world is defined by your personal view. Paradoxically, the surrender I am suggesting is about giving up this worldview. Surrender your notions of the word *surrender* to open a door of new meaning, a door to freedom, for surrender is just another word for true compassion. They are inseparable.

When I enter the Circle with someone and mention the idea of surrender their posture visibly stiffens. They may already be in a kind of warrior pose with arms akimbo and this pose will become stronger. Or if they are anchored in their *victim*, their hands may be in their pockets and they smile stiffly. They stiffen with suspicion because for them this word invokes an idea born from an old story. To them surrender means surrendering to an enemy. It means being powerless and helpless in the face of an adversary. They did not struggle and overcome great odds just so they could surrender while they are with me. This is a key moment. This is the moment in which they either decide to align themselves with what has been defining their worldview, running their Circle, so to speak, or to make a new choice for peace and freedom, and align themselves with the greater Circle of who they are.

This fear is born from the *idea* of the soldier's surrender, the surrender of one who fights and struggles for freedom, for the right to be, for worthiness, for honor, and for all the attributes of the indomitable warrior. This is not the meaning of the surrender I am suggesting you invoke. This is the idea of *surrender* coupled with the word *defeat*. The warrior is an idea we ride like a horse. In reality, it rides us ... or rather, it runs us and it will also run our Circle as a great controlling force. The same is true with the victim.

How does the warrior, the relentlessly brave doer, surrender his doing? Doing and thinking are the great addictions of both the warrior and the victim. To be quiet, to do nothing, to give up what you have spent your whole life cultivating as an identity driven by old stories, can seem like an impossible idea to the warrior and the victim. And how do you surrender when faced with a great challenge to your peace, happiness, and well-being? How can someone suffering with cancer even entertain the word *surrender*? How does a person sit with the word *surrender* when they are living with serious physical injury, then work and sweat through the pain for years to rehabilitate themselves only to find they must endure chronic pain for the rest of their lives?

My use of these words, *warrior* and *victim*, carry no judgment. They are neither bad nor good. But it's important to know that in their polarized state they function from survival and control. They are both dots in the Circle, which when balanced in their positive contributions serve the Circle of *you*, where they can align with the spine of your life and support the gift of *you*. But their unintegrated emotional history must be surrendered to the Circle so these positive forces can be liberated. This is the *surrender* I speak of.

Surrender is a word and words have vibration and power. Even words or phrases from other languages that you

Surrender

don't know the meaning of can fill you with peace and sacredness. *Surrender* has a unique sound and feeling to it. The syllables lead you forward into their essence: the soft *sur* glides into *ren* and then a solid grounding that enters as you touch the *d* and stand at the center in *der*. *Surrender* is an action and a sound that homes in on the center of the labyrinth; and if you can follow it, it guides you effortlessly through the unknown to your deepest *heartfelt* truth. The *surrender* I am talking about is another way to approach what it means to love yourself. It is another way to describe being the Circle to everything that moves.

In the Medicine of One, *surrender* refers to the hardened idea of who you think you are, whether we are referring to the victim or the warrior. You surrender this idea. You give it up; yet, you still honor your terror and rage, through the true action of self-love. This is a rooting in the Oneness, which allows opposites and contraries to move as part of the *flow* of this world and this life.

In this allowing and honoring you do not follow the thoughts and beliefs that can accompany the emotion. In fact, you must go even further and surrender your righteousness. You must give up being right. There is no such thing as being right. This rightness or righteousness can have an absolute feeling about it. So I call it *being right*. But hidden underneath it is the *need* to be right. *I am right* is just a *thought*. It's not the *truth*. If it is the truth how can there be a *greater* truth, which we all agree upon unconditionally? To give up *being right* is to give up believing in the thinking that holds a position. Honoring your own inner truth and integrity doesn't mean you have to be right in the view of others and the world. If you *need* to be right in the eyes of others to feed your sense of value and worth, then your truth becomes sourced outside of you. Honoring your own truth and integrity is the act of valuing yourself that really has no relationship to what others think.

The Medicine of One is a life path that leads to the center of *you*. I have described this journey over and over. It is so simple. But because it's not easy, we have to look at it from many different points of view. So this first act of surrender is simply an honoring of the *fragileness* within you. Surrender is a gradual path that uses your loving awareness, without judgment, in relationship to all that moves within you. It's important to kinesthetically know how surrender is married to compassion. They both melt to the ground from the center and expand spaciously as the Circle with your very breath.

Surrender, as a path, is the ability to give up your little **i** to the big **I** and finally to the infinite without years of struggle and search. This can be instantaneous and irreversible. This is usually the effortless route of the most enlightened humans who have come to us to teach us the path to our truth. For some reason the willful drive of survival, and its desires and needs was no match for the deeper current of desiring truth, freedom, and pure peace for them. They were able to surrender to the current that brought them into true knowing. What they surrendered was their thinking and the false sense of knowing that is born from that thinking. For them this was instantaneous. From this surrender their true purpose and spine of their life flowered effortlessly and radiated to others. In surrender their gift to the world was as simple as their *beingness*. But it was still their unique gift, still the thrust of *the spine of their life*. Even though these *enlightened ones* taught and functioned from what they called the absolute reality, there will never be anyone quite like them to walk the planet again.

There is a slower form of surrender, which is a path rather than an instantaneous moment of transformation. This second route *I* call the Medicine of One. It's the cultivation of your knowing presence as compassion as you direct your attention to the source of knowledge, which is a *knowing*. We have already established that this *knowing* is equivalent to *I don't know*. This is why this path is often called the path of self-knowledge and was greatly simplified by Ramana Maharshi as the Path of Self-Inquiry.

As you walk this path you will keep bumping into *who you are not* and surrender it slowly. But it's still *surrender*. It just placates the mind ... relaxes it so it can learn to step out of the way ... out of the little **i** with a dot toward the big **I** of the Circle ... so you are not identified with the dot, your thinking

Surrender

head. It is giving up the idea of you as the *doer*. Because we are all so mind driven, the bulk of humanity that seeks this *true self* with earnestness must travel the long route until they are finally able to surrender the mind that needs to know. In this way you surrender your *worldview*.

Ram Dass, American contemporary spiritual teacher and the author of *Be Here Now* published in 1971, suffered a stroke at 67. Suddenly he was in a wheel chair and forced to rely on others for help. Yet, he went on to write another book called, *Still Here: Embracing Aging, Changing and Dying*. This stroke created physical handicaps he embraced as his *teacher*. Years after he published his "Be Here Now", the stroke, as his teacher, taught him true *surrender*.

Sometimes life deals us a humbling hand of cards that is either temporary or ongoing. This is the critical moment and time when you must choose to live in the center and as the Circle of compassion for your warrior and your victim. This is the critical moment when you choose suffering, or you choose the compassion that is the refusal to suffer for imaginary reasons. Because no matter what the challenge, your mind will likely propel itself into the future owned by fear and worry, unless you choose to compassionately anchor yourself in something beyond your thinking.

There are very few people who have not had to face a great challenge at some point in their lives. I have chosen to share some of these moments in my own life because I feel it's important you know the place from which I speak. I have known days where it seemed as if I were dying. Partly physical in that I could not move well and barely seemed to care for my daily needs. This was not from illness but from my spinal problems, which can mimic many forms of debility. Within this debility is also a formidable mental weakening and emotional fragility. These are difficult times in which to remember the truth of who I am. It is hard to find that ever-present quiet. It is as if what I have come to experience as the truth of who I am disappears. The disabled body and mind want to claim my awareness and fill this space with their needs. In these times the best I can do is wait with the firm belief that it will pass and that I am far more than this desire to feel better and the fear of never coming out of it. The best I can do in that moment is to lie down into the arms of the quiet and do nothing. Life grounded in the *flow* is a balance between this *doing* and *being*.

I wonder in these times about the day that comes when it does not pass and I am lying in this Circle of who I am with my dogs, my ever present sentries, awaiting my movements and I cannot move. How will I feed them? Or myself? Because we have chosen this solitude that brings solidarity with all life, the practicality of someone to aid us in this dying will not be here. And we are all dying. It's just a question of the rate at which our bodies use themselves up and surrender its elements back to their elemental source. If there is fear, this too I must bring into the Circle. Rather than harden to my fear, I soften to it, and in that softening I am able to surrender to the arms of the Medicine of One.

Life is always challenging our survival. It is difficult to give up defining ourselves through this physical/mental/ emotional medium. It is difficult to give up the stories that have shaped us. As much as we want to be free of them, we can't stop thinking of them because of the unmoved, abandoned movements within us. So it is imperative they be brought back into the Circle of the greater you.

These are the difficult moments of surrender. These are the moments when the balance between *doing* and *being* must be invoked. To push with the *doer* can bring more suffering. That which challenges our ability to literally function in the world can be the most terrifying and perhaps the most liberating. It doesn't mean you are never afraid. It means you are not owned by that fear. Survival and fear are not the prime movers in the Circle of who you are, robbing you of peace and condemning you to roam in search of home. It means never forgetting that this truth of who you are is the *ever present home*. We can forget so easily. Especially, when our ability to bring our attention to this home seems impossible and we wander in the hell of our own mental world, populated with the lost and abandoned. It is we who have abandoned them in our attempt to throw them out of the Circle.

Begin to inquire *what am I defending?* Begin to inquire *who am I?* Begin to remember what is real. What is this sensa-

Surrender

tion of presence from which my world unfolds, from which my thoughts are generated, from which my pain and suffering are born? What lurks there beneath the *thinker* and the *doer*? Is it the little **i** who runs my Circle?

If you have a strong warrior in your Circle, his/her tight grip around fear becomes gently opened in the quest for truth, which is in part the giving up of the untruth of who you think you are. No longer do you assume ... *this is who I am.* Now it is *who am I?* Ponder the difference. Let life be the teacher that opens you to the true possibility of you. No matter how difficult your past or present, resist blaming and jumping on the spinning wheel of your story that never stops. Stop repeating your story. Find out who it is that keeps believing the story and keeps it alive by completely rejecting the victim feelings from the stance of the warrior, or who indulgently swims in them as the drowning victim. In this path of self-knowledge you choose to use life as that which helps you remember this feeling of *who am I,* rather than the forgetting of the stubborn dead-end path of survival.

I know what this *forgetting* is like. I have lived it. Now there is no other path for me but the path of the Circle, this Medicine of One. When you can get over the idea of *giving up* as being defeat, then there really *is* no giving up, only giving *in* to the quiet presence that waits. Too much time without the quiet and I lose myself in the noise of everyday life, which in one form or another is all born from my mind.

I know it's not easy. It's simple, but far from easy. The times we need to remember the most are the times when it is the hardest. That is why this remembering must be practiced and strengthened until it is second nature and then finally first nature. This is why, although I help people *clear the way*, sharing the Medicine of One is the most important thing I do. We don't really need to fix anything, just surrender an old stubborn habit of survival, and walk through life with a new relationship to the life within us and without.

Give up importance. Give up unimportance. Give up worrying and not worrying. Give up to give in. Just give it up. If you simply can't, then be this Medicine of One to whatever clings. Whatever cannot, will not give up. Be love to your *I can't,* in its movement of desperate rage. Allow this energy of desperate rage to move through your whole body and become the giving up and giving in, and *clear the way.* The greatest of all fears and threats, *the great nothing,* must be stared in the face. Look into the mirror of truth, which reflects no history, ideas, or notions of truth and importance, and see only imageless light reflected back, as if you were staring into the face of the sun.

Knowing what I have said may give you the patience to wait for peace, but it alone won't give you that peace. You must spend time in the true Circle of who you are. You must water this garden of the heart with your soft attention. You must sit and be quiet often, or carry the same sense of stillness while in movement. Don't wait. Your own beautiful peace is right there, in this moment, silently waiting for you.

Chapter Seventeen

Prayer and Faith

Let your praying be an active state of surrender.
Let it be true communion.

Prayer is very personal. It is an intimate bond between you and a Higher Power and Presence that you have faith in. This intimacy has no barrier, no separation. Faith gives us the ability to enter the state of prayer. I have great faith in the truth of my presence as compassion. Doubtlessly, I sit in communion with this greater presence and this for me is prayer. Like a church, the Circle is a sacred place that helps me touch my faith and enter the state of prayer:

> *You can hear the singing sound of silence*
> *You can smell the juniper all wet with rain*
> *In the forests of ponderosa and painted deserts*
> *It's a religion without a name"*
>
> From the song *Arizona*
> Lomakayu

This vast land is both my church and my bible. It speaks to me, it teaches me, and it leads me into the *Holy presence of the quiet One* that I am. True faith is quiet trust. When you can't trust, you think a lot trying to create faith and trust through your thinking. It's the mind's survival drive, which functions from "If I can control the outcome, I can have peace and then I can have faith." Contemplate this: Is prayer wanting

Medicine of One

something or is prayer communion and surrender?

One day I was at one of my Circles sharing its essence and meaning with someone. My dogs, Cheyenne and Hanta Yo, sat quietly in the shade of the Circle and gifted us with their presence. We closed our eyes for a long moment and listened to the Holy Being of the Wind. Because that long moment was simply sitting in the *now*, it could have been five minutes or twenty. When we rose to leave, Cheyenne and Hanta Yo were gone. The Circle was on top of a mesa. I walked around its edge looking out across the land for miles in all directions, and crisscrossed its breadth searching for them. My voice rang out over the desert calling to them. I saw nothing. We waited for a while ... and still nothing. I decided to leave a blanket in the Circle with a bowl of water. I had responsibilities to the person I was with. I trusted that the bowl and blanket would tell the dogs I was coming back if they returned to the Circle. We journeyed to another sacred place and on our way back I stopped and walked back to the Circle again and roamed the mesa ... still nothing.

When you let your animals live as free spirits this is always the chance you take. You have given up control and their wolf spirits love to explore and chase other animals. Big game runs fast and long distances. In this area they probably caught the scent of a herd of antelope. I breathed into a tense movement inside of me. I knew if I fed it with fearful thoughts it could escalate into panic, so we went back to the truck and drove back to my house where my client's car was.

Once we said goodbye, I headed back to the Circle. It was one of those days blessed by a deep blue sky contrasted with white cottony clouds. There is profoundness when moments of urgency occur in the infinite beauty of the desert. I drove very slowly scanning off to the distance on each side of the road. Nothing was moving out there, not even a bird or a jackrabbit. I arrived back at the Circle and found it just as I had left it, empty. I lie down on my back on the blanket, looking up at the sky and softly felt my worry, my previous memories of loss, my helplessness, and my smallness within this vast Circle.

There is a delicate balance between surrender and doing everything you can in these moments. Obviously, I could

Prayer and Faith

not have stayed home believing they would somehow find their way back. It was ten or fifteen miles out in the wilderness with dangerous highways, cattle ranches, and cowboys protecting their cattle who would not hesitate to shoot a dog trying to down one of their cows. I knew all the possibilities but stayed in the center of the Circle without getting involved in what the mind can create, which can fan the flame of fear.

But I could not deny my fear, and as I lay on my back I breathed and let all those fears move through my very body and the Circle. I let the tears roll warmly down my cheeks. As I lay there held by the earth I just felt Cheyenne and Hanta Yo in my arms licking my face. I felt their wet tongues and furry scent.

There was still one last effort I needed to make. I drove up a winding dirt road to a panorama of the land below, where the Circle was a dot in the great Circle. My eyes slowly traveled back and forth searching for any kind of movement ... nothing. The sun was touching Mingus Mountain in the distance and would disappear very soon. There was nothing more I could do. I had searched without giving up. I had laid in surrender in the Circle and my prayer, which was the feeling of Cheyenne and Hanta Yo in my arms, had been set into movement like a bottle with a note in the sea of the vastness.

I drove back, still searching the road for any movement. Just as I was approaching a cattle guard, which was the beginning of civilization and a different kind of danger, I glanced off to my left and there they were, winding their way toward me through a maze of arroyos. I jumped out of the car and met them half way. I felt their warm panting on me as I hugged them, and I let my angry frustration tremble down through my legs as gratitude filled me.

This is a story of what prayer is to me. It answers the question, "What about prayer in the Circle?" Is the Circle a place to go and pray? If you create a Circle, that Circle is *your* sacred space. No one can tell you how to use it. I can only share my own world, what the Circle means to me, and what I do when I enter it.

Rather than become involved in words and thinking, I enter the Circle, and surrender everything that is moving inside of me to the greater compassion that I am. Into the arms of this compassion I give up control, but I also plant the seed of a good outcome in the Circle from which all creation sprouts. I might plant that seed with an intention that aligns me with how I wish to live. I might use a few words to empower it such as, "Let me serve the greater good," or "Let me do the best I can today." I place these words of direction into the Circle of who I am and then just let it be done, and then I get out of the way. Prayer for me is no different than entering the silent presence that brings me into Godliness: a listening, absorbed in my own immediate present *hereness* that is all allowing and has no judgment. Praying is a movement, which steps into the flow of life, whose current communes with the great mystery that is called God.

We often pray when something happens, and we feel powerless and helpless when it seems it's beyond the efforts of our will. We often pray because we want something. We want everything to be all right. We want to be well if we are sick. We want a friend who is dying before us to go on living. If they are in pain we want them to be free of this pain. We helplessly watch them twisting, turning, and grimacing in physical pain.

Since you are not separate from this great *One* and you are the creator in your own universe, asking for something to be given to you from a force that is separate from you creates division. Rather, feel the outcome in you, in your Circle, and in the ones you love. Feel it as already done. But let what you pray for be free of your little **i**'s willful needs and illusions. If you need more money, feel abundance raining down from the sky. If it's for better health and healing, feel peace, harmony, balance and trust, and surrender to the Circle as to how that outcome will manifest. Or if in the moment of losing a loved one you miss them and feel an aloneness descending upon you, give your *missing* and *aloneness* to the Circle. Surrender it so that in this *moment of undeniable dying* and the approach of death you can become the peace that you want, that you would verbally pray for on behalf of the one you love who is leaving.

Prayer, for me, and even some of the ancient silent traditions of Christianity, is about entering a quiet state of surrender. There may be a movement in my Circle, which desires

Prayer and Faith

a blessed outcome for myself or for others. For instance, "I want my animal friends to come home to me." I can't deny this. But, I cannot allow this wanting to be driven by panic. So I bring everything I could possibly be feeling into the Circle, the Circle that I am, that is greater than this story. And with my very breath I become this Circle to all that moves within me. I do not get involved in thinking whether it is worrisome or in projecting a positive outcome and explanation. If I get involved in the thinking then I have allowed this story to own me. I have allowed myself to be swept into the spin. I have forgotten who I really am. This is a state of wanting and separation.

If your prayer and desire is for connection and peace, this kind of prayer state is the doorway to what you want. Hear your own *hereness* ... touch it with the attentive hand of the mind. Beyond that felt presence that you are, beyond that surrender to the silence, beyond no thought, nothing can be said ... not even that it is God. Let your praying be an active state of surrender. Let it be *true communion.*

Medicine of One

Chapter Eighteen

Flow

*You too are of the beauty of this earth.
Listening to the ground of your being
brings you into relationship with Holy Being
so you may go with the flow.*

Commit to making this journey as *flow*, like the flow of the river from the mountains to the sea, rarely holding a straight course, but following a hidden path of least resistance. Strong, persistent ... but constantly giving up your thinking mind's *I know this is the way* so you can touch the flow with your deep listening. This is as if the water itself were listening to the wisdom of the ground to a route laid down in the millenniums of creation. Listening is the way of *flow* ... listening with an ear to the ground of your being.

This beautiful earth is the flow made visible. This includes everything that moves upon it as well as the still quiet places that call us. A sacred place on the land is far more than its components of rocks, trees, dirt, sky, light, and water. Places have a presence. The Navajos believe certain formations have a Holy Being *bii'istíín* who resides in sacred places and formations and is very important in their stories of the land. This Holy Being is an experience of a presence that emerges from the *flow*. The wind is also a Holy Being known as *Niłch'i Diyin* that has a presence that is not just air blowing. This presence manifests as a sound in the trees and plants, clouds moving, the soft warm touch of the wind on your face, force, and direction. The Holy Being of the wind is not something composed of its parts. It's a kind of poetics of space that emerges from *the flow*, meaning it all points to something beyond, a presence unnamable but felt as a kind *being*.

The river is more than a metaphor. It's a teacher. The *flow of One* is a song, a symphony of *being* that is water moving over the land, the flight of cliff swallows, ravens, hawks, the movement of air rippling the water, dragon flies, gnats, bees, sky, and clouds ... what speaks from the *being of river* is endless. Water is just one elemental movement in this *flow of One*. So *the river is a Holy Being that transcends the obvious flow of water*. I have used this *river* in a dual sense. It began as a metaphor to discuss *the flow*. But the river is part of the deeper flow of One. Its r*esonant being* can lead you into the flow.

Whether you are aware of it or not, you too are part of this flow of *Holy Beingness*. You too are the *flow* made visible. You too are of the beauty of this earth. Listening to the ground of your being brings you into relationship with Holy *Being* so you may *go with the flow*.

The way home to the sea is a flow, not a fight, as effortless as water flowing downhill and surrendering to the knowing of gravity itself. "But sometimes we have to struggle" you say, "Sometimes we have to fight." Yes, but even in this movement of determination you can listen to the ground, you can move forward without righteousness and violence. You can still honor the sanctity of life, stay grounded in the heart, and live in a flow of generosity to yourself and to others.

Flow is the opposite of how most of us have survived. You may have been fortunate to have parents who lived and demonstrated that *flow*. But still it is almost impossible to avoid painful experiences in life. When it happens in childhood we often don't know what's happening. It doesn't *feel good* though. All of us want to be happy and feel good. In this pursuit of happiness we reject the feelings that don't feel good, unknowingly rejecting some of the energetics of our own truth. In this effort to avoid the hurt and the pain we dam the *flow*. We gradually move out of the *magical flow* of our true being.

There are many whose trauma and pain are not so subtle and hidden. How do you *flow* when someone is beating you? How do you *flow* when your father sneaks into your bed in the middle of the night and you are sworn to secrecy? How do you *flow* when a schoolyard of children humiliate you so

Flow

harmfully that you would rather be dead than suffer their hateful stares and cruelty? How do you *flow* when as a child your family is slaughtered in front of you? There are scarring moments in our *soul's history* when *flow* was impossible. This is true. We all have them. The emotions we blocked in our drive to survive and some of the beliefs we adopted to aid our survival separates us from the *flow*. What stands in the way? How do we return home to this *flow*?

This journey is not without obstacles. But sometimes when we think we are being slowed by a detour, it becomes evident that the detour was the way. For without that experience the next one could not follow. One leads to the next and sometimes it's only when we pause and look back, thankful for where we are, we know it was all for a reason.

Waiting in the *flow* is our own soul medicine ready for us to call it forth. If you are reading this book you have made it through the impossible and now it's time for peace and to live as *flow*. I did not say *the* flow. I said *flow*. This is a living wisdom. This is truth. There is no *the* before it. *Flow* is no different than being. *Being* is not "a" or "the" *being*. It is simply *being*.

You cannot make two into one. You must be the ONE it all moves in. *Flow* is moving through the world of duality connected to that ONE that you are. *Flow* is a great trust in a *knowing prior to thought, prior to what you believe.* It is from the sense of *flow* and listening that a trusting faith can come. To enter this *flow* is to give up being the *doer* who accomplishes and the thinker who knows: to give up the one who succeeds, and the one who fails. It's giving up good and bad, right and wrong. It's giving up your investment in a world of duality. It's giving up believing in your thinking. It's giving up being right. It's giving up this little **i** so you may enter the *flow* of the big **I**, the *flow* between heaven and earth, and the *flow* where all opposites are one *flow*. You root in it as the Circle of compassion.

How do you find this *flow* when your life habit is the opposite? When everything I am talking about seems so far away? You are already closer to it having come this far. Just start walking the path. Don't worry that you wander off at

Medicine of One

times. Just decide you are here to be peace, and let the *great mystery channel through you* as the unique expression that is the *you in this world*.

The Medicine of One is a path to enter the *flow of one*, which looks to the world around us to teach and guide us. We just have to look. We just have to feel the wind. Feel the river, the ocean. Come. Feel the tree, the hawk. Then feel them as a guide to the mystery of the flow that is the *mystery of You*. But you must give your attention to it. You must regain your listening and give attention to the flow.

There is a truth relative to this dream world. If there wasn't we would have no way to find our bearings. When we gaze at the night sky to find our way as we sail across the vast ocean, the truth of the star's position is relative to us. But we can use that truth in this dream world to navigate what seems like endless water to arrive at a destination. Ultimately, the knowing I am speaking of is like a bird sensing the magnetic North and knowing which direction to fly in. Somehow, someway it *hones* in with uncanny precision and a Zen-like release of the arrow from the bow, which finds the bull's eye in surrender to the *now*.

It is from the sense of *flow* and listening that a trusting faith can come. The only fear that is a problem is the unseen repressed one. That which is not seen claims ownership of your mind. We use our minds in a different way to pass through the doorway into the Medicine of One. Rather than use our minds to wrestle with our fear, we direct the attention of our minds to become as big as the sky to the movement of thoughts.

You have to sense it with total attention. Books, teachers, and wisdom of the ages can point the way. What I am writing can point the way. But it isn't a thought or something that happens through constantly repeating it to yourself or reading it over and over again from one book or another. You have to seek it as a stalker, with keen attention and listening with the whole of you. You have to *BE the Listening*. And if you don't know what that means, you have to find out what that means. And when you find out ... when you taste it ... touch it ... you must practice it as effortlessly as possible. Surrender

Flow

your mind to the listening, to this presence, which is pre-sense, before the senses determine what you give your attention to.

Trapped in our stories by the wall of emotion held together by belief separates us from the *flow*. The Medicine of One for me is a way to immediately touch this *flow* and invoke it as the Holy Being of the Circle, which is *you*, your Holy Being, to gently soften the wall and liberate the energies that have been separated from the *flow*.

Perhaps you are already on the river past midway, right where it's the most difficult. It's too late to turn back, but you still can't see the shore. If you can give up all of your expectations, hopes, and dreams ... then all that remains is giving up your belief of impossible, hopeless, disbelief, doubt, distrust, and self-deprecation. Just give up both of these realms of illusion ... give up believing in the cement of your beliefs that has hardened around the stones of your pain. Why hang on to beliefs that take you to the bottom of the river? Give up believing in the impossible and the possible, and be the *flow* that is the river of life. If you can give up hopes and dreams then give up the opposite as well. Give up all illusion and float on what is real. There never was a bank of the river that you left and there is not a bank of the river on the other side. All you have to do is stop believing what you think. If you find you keep flipping from one extreme to the other, then stand in the middle, don't grab ahold of any of it as it passes you by, and walk on water. Let the greater power we all move in flow through you. Surrender the thought *I know* ... and *flow*.

Medicine of One

Chapter Nineteen

The Magic of Soul Medicine

Soul Medicine is anything that creates a bridge for your awareness to cross and allow you to embrace your deep soulful being with the compassion of the Circle.

Give up judging, analyzing, and labeling. Give it up and live in the *flow of magic and wonder.* The true illusion is what you think you know. To live each day as *I don't know* is to meet that day fresh and let its wonder speak to you. Allowing meaningfulness without holding fast to what exactly that meaningfulness means is to enjoy this beautiful, earthly life as that which is true, rather than accepting the common labels of so called reality as truth and most especially those labels that apply to you.

If *our world is our own private dream* and *reality is our quiet presence* does this mean that the beauty and magic, which come to us in everyday life, are to be discounted? Are these wonderful gifts just our imagination? The answer is no. Moving in this world, knowing this world is a dream and everyone's dream is different, does not imply our experience is meaningless. It simply means the meaning of this world comes from us.

The *flow* is the place where magic springs forth into the world of time. But the *flow* itself is timeless because it is where everything is connected. Magic bridges the two worlds of the visible and the invisible, and having come *out* of the *flow* it takes you back *into* the *flow*. From this *flow*, the magic can speak to you in the form of an ancestral being in the clouds at the moment when you sit in timelessness. It can stir your depths when a butterfly lands on your sleeve or when an emotional burden, which has weighed you down for lifetimes, lifts, tipping the scales that bring you into balance and harmony. You can be jettisoned into a timeless moment as you stop along the side of the road to cry and see a bright red rose in a dead tree with the profound feeling that it was placed there just for you.

These moments are like **Messengers of Synchronicity** and can be anything that comes into your awareness that rings with a resonance, which makes you stop, pause, and breathe in the magic ... the *magic*. These profound messengers can touch you in an indescribable way with a feeling that shimmers through you. They take you into the flow where you can only smile and say "Wow!" Synchronicity allows for the osmotic exchange between our soulful, multidimensional, imaginative being and this solid, three-dimensional, sometimes unimaginative material world.

The world is not time bound. *We* bind it to the cycles of time. Nature itself lives in eternity, ever in flux on the surface but forever born from unbound Oneness. This is why nature is such a potent doorway to our true self.

By consciously choosing to be open to the flow, the magic can happen in a flash of spontaneity or we can more deliberately invoke the magic. The objects, events, and words that effortlessly come to us to deliver these energies can heal both our ancient and current emotional pains or touch us with a wonder that bridges the invisible and visible worlds I call *soul medicine*.

Soul medicine is soul magic. It speaks to you in the language of the soul through the energies of symbolism, metaphor, synchronicity, and the sheer poetry of life. This language emerges from the flow. Soul medicine speaks in the language of soul and stirs whatever needs to move for freedom and peace. It can heal your rejected pain and liberate you from an old story. But *soul medicine* may also bring you into the pure joy of life in the moment it happens, or spark a revelation in your *knowing*. Its very nature is a mystery because it speaks *from* the mystery and touches the mystery of your soul. It's virtually anything that creates a bridge for your awareness to cross and

The Magic of Soul Medicine

allows you to embrace your deep, soulful being with the compassion of the Circle.

Allow its forms to be limitless. Find out for yourself what soul medicine is. Write in the margins of this book and fill in the blanks. Every one of us is different ... so is the meaningfulness that touches us.

Sometimes when I am working with people I ask them to gather all manner of physical objects to give form to any aspect of their story. I call this process **Gathering Soul Medicine**. Gathering physical objects helps people to move out of their analytical mind into their *feeling* body and truly engage the energies of their feelings. When you surrender to your intention and bring back into the Circle what you have cast out, you are dialoguing with flow. Your intention calls forth what you need as the medicine to heal your soul's forgotten pain. In this process you gather Soul Medicine through consciously intending, as you walk, to pick up objects which could be anything from a piece of dried up cow dung, a broken stick, a daisy, or a piece of shattered glass. These objects will speak in a variety of ways to different people. In the beginning, gathered objects can appear as something you don't like and yet if you can bring them into the Circle they hold a gift. People are consciously choosing to bring back into the Circle the rejected, abandoned, and imprisoned emotional forces in their soul's history that still remain unintegrated. This *act of gathering* leads people to their own self-compassion. These *unwanted children of our feelings* become the *soul medicine* that frees something positive inside of them. Our disowned pain, when honored with breath and love, is a medicine that brings us back into balance, harmony and freedom.

One day I was walking with a man named Jeremy along the Verde River. I had explained the Circle and the Medicine of One to him. I wanted him to gather, in the form of anything that spoke to him, *all* that which needed to be brought back into the Circle of his love. I told him to place the intention into his heart to gather the lost and forgotten in his soul's journey through experience.

They could be any objects, which reminded him of people who have hurt him. They could embody himself at a particular age or any object that embodied frozen feelings of rage, terror, sadness, or grief ~ any feelings that might still be unmoved in his history. "Don't think, don't analyze, don't make a list," I told him. "Pick up whatever captures your attention and immediately trust your first impulse. Do not listen to your doubting mind, which can seem much louder than this silent impulse that stirs in you."

He spent an hour wandering around the rocky flood plain of the river. This was an area also frequented by people searching for a cool place in the heat of the desert. They often left their garbage and belongings behind. One of the objects he collected was an old white sock caked with mud. I knew immediately what it embodied but I didn't want to say anything until we went to the sacred Circle, which was a fifteen-minute drive from our location on the river. As we drove to the Circle, I asked him to be particularly gentle with the sock and that somehow its dirty, homeless, cast off state was reaching out to him.

When we walked into the Circle and I asked Jeremy to sweep the ground with a branch of the desert broom bush to establish the Circle as being his for that day. He had gathered a number of objects, but the sock was the key. I let him work his way up to the sock. He looked at it and started to cry. He told me as a child his abusive mother had made him wear socks for gloves to school. This sock was both his great shame and his great rage. He shook with tight tears as if he were tensing around them. Softly, in the background, I encouraged Jeremy to breathe and be the Circle to his child self. He inhaled deeply and exhaled a deep sigh ... in seconds his last tear touched the earth. Once a peace settled over him, I told him that was enough for the day. I wanted him to sit with this and let these feelings move, along with any other memories that might come to him.

"Whatever you feel, give it your loving breath ... soften to it ... and carry that sock reverently back to your room ... wash it carefully and let it dry." I said.

He nodded his head and said, "Thanks Lomakayu. I already feel ... different. I can't really explain it."

"Don't try," I said and I gave him a big hug.

The Magic of Soul Medicine

The next day Jeremy and I returned to the Circle. We had honored his shame and hurt the day before. Today was about letting his *hurt* find transformation through the fire of his rage. Now another kind of magic was invoked through the very instrument of life and feeling ... the body. Through the mystery of physical gesture and voice, we cleared the way. Everything speaks to help deliver the perfect *feeling form,* words, tone, and volume that if entered and surrendered to, will liberate the imprisoned life within. I call these sound filled forms **primordial movements.** *They* appear to me *in the moment* in my mind just like the sock appeared to Jeremy. These primordial movements can, in an instant, bridge the world of opposites that have been separated such as *the warrior and the victim.* This bridging is the way back into the flow.

I demonstrated a helpless reaching out, filled with the pleading words, "Mom." I did not tell him it was himself as a child or instruct him in any other way. Jeremy immediately did as I had showed him. I told him to relax and breathe. Jeremy cried and trembled just like the day before. And then I immediately had him stomp on the ground, driving his fists straight down, looking straight ahead, and screaming with the intent to kill, yelling, "Mom!!!" At first he closed his eyes, internalizing and driving the force inward, which completely altered the energy being invoked. This was where he was stuck in a rage toward himself. The rage we needed to invoke was outward moving. I had him do the sequence again with open eyes. The same tears shook through him as the previous day, only this time they came out of his rage. They were hot with fire and strength. These feelings flowed through him very quickly and were followed by calmness. I asked him to extend his arms out to the sides, palms down, at shoulder level, feeling anchored and grounded and from that energy speak his own name. He said "Jeremy!" with worth, value, confidence, strength, and courage. This was an energy he had never known. He became quiet, still, and as solidly rooted as a tree.

Just then, the shadow of a big bird passed through the Circle and when we looked up we saw a huge turkey vulture gliding over us as if acknowledging the moment. People sometimes have a negative idea attached to vultures. To me they recycle and transform what has died. You will frequently see them picking at road kill of a rabbit, coyote, or skunk. The appearance of the vulture made the moment even more profound. We both stood there *anchored in the timeless quiet of the flow.*

The sock, the primordial movement, and the vulture were different forms of Soul Medicine that came from the flow because we called to it and then listened. These movements helped clear the way for Jeremy back into the flow of One. He built a fire and burned the sock as a reflection of his own liberated fire. He transformed his shame and freed himself of an old belief that had haunted him as a voice questioning his worth. A beautiful liberating moment doesn't have to be the witnessing of physical beauty.

Sometimes the gift of Soul Medicine is difficult medicine to swallow. If you can swallow it and relax as the Circle of compassionate presence, the ashes from the fire of change will pass through you like a vulture gliding through the sky. Fire returns the elements to the earth where they emerge from the flow in a new form. No longer believing in his shame, Jeremy allowed new qualities of his presence to come from his sense of confidence and worth. This happened easily and effortlessly because he was back in the flow. That dirty old sock had come out of the flow as a magical gift to help him connect with trapped energies within. The sock, by taking him into the energy of his past pain, transcended its usefulness as a metaphor. As a metaphor it was simply food for the linear mind. The soul is part of the flow and we needed to speak the language of *soul* and *flow* ~ e-motion, energy in motion.

I will share another one of these magical times that came because of the intent of the day, which was *freedom*. For three days I had been working with Lois, who had a very traumatic past and whose way of dealing with it was to dissociate. She also had a lot of underlying panic. We headed out into the wilderness in my truck. As we were driving down the road, a small bird dove in front of the truck and disappeared. I looked in the rearview mirror and saw it lying there in the road still moving a bit. The air current had probably sucked it under the car. I turned around and went back. The bird was lying in the

The Magic of Soul Medicine

middle of the road on its back, barely moving, but without any apparent injuries. I picked it up and got into the truck. It lay in the palm of my hand on its back. I stroked its head and neck until it kind of sat up in my hand. I felt it would be important for Lois to hold the bird, so I offered it to her. She looked at me fearfully and said, "I'm afraid of birds." I said, "Okay," and the bird fluttered out of my hand into the back where the dogs were and of course they were very eager to claim it. It managed to hide underneath the seat. The bird fluttered in the truck as if banging into the walls of a cage, while the dogs excitedly tried to grab ahold of it with open jaws. I got out, pulled the seat up, picked up the bird, and held it out to the open sky. It flew off. Then Lois explained that it was trapped birds that frightened her, the way they bounce off the windows and walls in a flutter of *panic*.

We had set out that day to gather Soul Medicine for her to bring into the sacred Circle, our final destination. How uncannily synchronistic and perfect it was for that bird to have offered itself in that miraculous way. I have never had this happen with a bird nor could I imagine someone could be frightened of birds. To have those two events come together in the same moment was just another example of the magic of it all. It does seem to happen a lot in different ways. But this one touched me deeply.

Soul medicine helps us to come back into balance and harmony so we can align with the *spine of our life* ~ our gift and the thrust of why we are here on the earth. My time with Jeremy and Lois concluded in a similar way with one last invocation of magic from the natural world. I asked them both to find a stick to embody the *spine of their life*. I told them, "It can be any piece of wood, straight as an arrow, curved like a flowing river, or split like a person dancing with legs spread like the roots of trees and arms reaching to the sky. It might look like a bird, a dragon, or a mythic creature of power. The stick used to embody your spine can be large and straight like a walking stick or a staff. The importance is that you are drawn to it. You like the feel of it and the energetic movement it seems to embody and express. When you see it, something in your heart knows ... *this is it.*"

Medicine of One

Both Jeremy and Lois had been looking for their stick after our first meeting. Jeremy found his on the first day when he found the sock. In fact it was very close to the sock. Almost as if saying, "Bring one in and the other follows." His spine stick looked like it had originally been part of a broom. The broom end was gone, but the staff of the broom was completely intact. Both ends were smooth and rounded, as was the whole stick, as if it had spent a lot of time journeying down the river that had carried his sock as well. It was perfectly straight and strong and appeared to have never been broken. This was Jeremy's new choice ~ although he had a story of his *worth* being broken, the spine of his life had never been broken. He could use it as a walking stick, but he found himself twirling it like a baton. In this action it embodied the freedom of his soul.

I asked Jeremy what kind of work he did. He said he was an artist and an art therapist. I asked him what he wanted his art to bring to people. He said healing. In sharing the vision of his own journey through pain, his intent was to awaken the *knowing* that they were not alone and their suffering's meaning was a journey to truth.

"What about your work as an art therapist?" I asked him.

He replied, "I wanted to help children overcome their trauma through their creativity."

Then I asked, "Aren't these two intents one and the same. Isn't there a single thrust of compassion at work here? Isn't there compassion toward your own paintings that touch and explore your pain, which extends out as a compassion for other's suffering? And isn't your compassion for these children the same force that inspires them to give meaning to their suffering to bring them into freedom?"

He thought about it for a moment and replied, "Yes."

"So let's see if we can refine the spine of your life into its simplest form. There is compassion, pain, and freedom. You want freedom for people. Tell me a little bit about the qualities of that freedom," I asked Jeremy.

"It's a freedom to be who you are, to express that," he answered.

"Is it full of the feeling of worth, value, and belief in

The Magic of Soul Medicine

themselves?" I asked.

"Absolutely. Yes, I want them to believe in themselves," he answered.

"You are empowering them?" I asked.

"Yes," he stated.

"Okay." I stood there quietly for a moment. "To be the compassion that inspires worth. To be compassionate inspiration that empowers. To be empowering compassion."

"Yes, yes, yes, the last one." He held his stick in the air.

I handed him a *Magic Marker*. "Write those words on the stick however you want. Spread it out over the whole stick. Let the words wrap around it. However you want to do it. Let this freedom begin now."

He decided, rather then stringing the words in a line, to write them at different angles, sizes, and script. He wanted each word, he said, to have its own sense of freedom.

"Perfect," I said. "*To be empowering* compassion is something *you are* before being something *you do*. It is what comes through you effortlessly when you live at the center of the Circle of who you are." I stood on the large center rock of the Circle. "And because it's something you are it radiates out and through you. You are this first for yourself. Everything we have done is really this action to yourself. You must *be it* for yourself so that you are demonstrating this empowering compassion. This will be your presence that inspires and silently touches others."

Then I stepped off the rock and gestured for Jeremy to step up holding his staff. "Engage this spine of your life and live from this and be aware when you stray especially in being it to yourself."

We stood there quietly for a moment. I picked up my flute and said, "Receive this as an honoring song for your courage in everything you have done here. Feel the wind honor you, feel the sun honor you, and feel my dogs, Cheyenne and Hanta Yo gazing with honor upon you." I played a song of honoring on the flute. Afterwards, Jeremy continued to stand there for a long time. I told him to stay there as long as he needed as I gathered my things. Cheyenne and Hanta Yo were halfway to the truck already. "I am going to leave you here alone. When you are complete, walk straight towards that tree." I pointed to a tall juniper in the distance, "And you'll see the truck in a straight line beyond it."

Lois didn't find her stick until we were completely finished and her anxiety had settled. In this settling, her knowing could come forth and her stick readily presented itself when she glanced in the shade of a tree where my wolf/dog, Beauty, was just starting to chew on it. Beauty delivered the final act of magic. She easily allowed Lois to pick it up and bring it into the Circle. Her spine stick was smooth, flowing and weightless. It had originally been a small branching root of a cottonwood tree. Weightlessness for Lois spoke of being free from the heavy anxiety that had plagued her all her life preventing her from living in the flow. She loved her stick. It excited her.

I had already spoken about the meaning of the stick and the essence of what the spine of her life was about. As we stood in the Circle she was beaming with a smile. " I already know what it is," she said. "It's the opposite of my anxiety. It's about flow and truth. I have never been able to be who I am. I have lived in constant worry, always thinking about what might happen to me. You can't flow that way."

I asked her, "Alright. When you daydream about doing something new through your work, what comes to you? What do you see?"

She hesitated. "I have always been afraid to say it. It's been there since I was a child. I see things about people that could help them. But everyone used to make fun of me. So I shut it down. I stopped trusting."

"Through this help to others, what do you want for them?" I asked Lois, "Through the use of your gift of counseling what do you want them to go away with?"

She took a while to answer me. "Peace ... I want them to have peace."

"So how might you engage these people with your words and presence to invoke peace?"

"Love. I want them to know they are loved," Lois answered.

"So the key words are love and peace?" I asked.

"Joy, too. Joy needs to be in there," she said.

The Magic of Soul Medicine

"Joyful peace?" I asked.

"Yes," she said.

"Can you put that all together, ideally beginning with *to be*, because it's something you are." She frowned at me as if stumped by my request. "Okay let me see if I can help you. If it doesn't ring true, don't agree with it. Begin now to honor your own sense of truth."

"Oh! I almost forgot about the truth part. That's important," she added.

I looked out over the desert and saw two ravens riding the up drafts of the wind. *Flow, truth, joy, peace, and love* I thought. "To be the flow of love that brings joyful peace ... to be peaceful joy ... to be the truthful flow of loving peace ... is the true flow full of love and peace?" I asked her.

She nodded her head, *yes*.

"To be the true flow that brings peaceful love ... to be the true flow of peace ... to be the ..."

"Yes ... that's it, that's it!" She jumped in gleefully, "*To be* the true flow of peace. Love is already in there." She grabbed the pen out of my hand and wrote it on her root stick.

"Beautiful, Lois, beautiful." She warmly placed her spine stick over her heart. I made one last request of her, "Be the true flow of peace to yourself always, to all that disturbs your peace. Be it first and let your *doing* come from this." I sang Amazing Grace in Cherokee as she stood there. *Everything finished well.*

Six months later Lois called to thank me. She was starting to see clients and had created a website to explain her mission and work.

When we discover the *spine of our life* we energize and honor it. Simple and clear, but poetic, the phrase invokes a magic, transcending the mind's linear way of understanding. Jeremy and Lois may like the spine of their life without fully understanding it. Understanding will come from *clearing the way to its truth* and being free from all the stories that would hold them back.

Awareness, openness, and participation in the *flow*, brings these occurrences and synchronicities out of the flow. It's as if we become a magnet for them. The more open and

Medicine of One

living in the flow we are the more we magnetize these happenings. The more *we notice* it, the more it will happen. You have opened the door to the *flow.* Even though that sock and the broomstick were man made objects forgotten and left behind as litter, their appearance was natural and unorchestrated; and the bird offering itself at that precise moment in our journey would be impossible to willfully create, as well as my wolf/dog Beauty's choosing Lois's stick.

Two Worlds ~ One Moment. Living in the flow effortlessly allows the natural world and our imagination to dance together. In this dance, *soul medicine* visits us with its gift of healing. We only have to receive the gift by feeling what it points the way to in an old story, where a part of us is still trapped.

So dance with the wind and sun, and step barefoot in *the river of the flow.* Be open and participate in that flow. Let life be meaningful. Let the magic speak to you. If you let it happen, if you listen . . . it *will* happen. It's always there. You just have to listen.

Chapter Twenty

Creativity is Married to the Spiritual Quest
Creativity can bring us into the moment of the Self. It can both free and invoke the soul

When I ask a question but don't rush in to fill the space with an answer, something happens in the silence. Something is invoked just by asking, but I must be still and feel it. When I ask the question "Who am I?" ... I feel the empty space of presence. This is the *Quiet One* and the answer to the question. *Medicine of One* has come forth into written form in this way. The final Chapter, *The Quiet One*, came first ~ as the expression of what is always eternally there. I knew this chapter was the end, but I had no idea what the journey to the Quiet One looked like. There was never an outline at any time. The writing of the *Medicine of One* has been a creative journey to the center.

In this moment I sit in the mystery of the Circle silently waiting. I sit as open space waiting for something to surface like a bubble of air floating up from the bottom of the sea. The Circle I am sitting in is at the edge of a cliff with a one hundred foot drop-off. A raven is far in the distance and flies straight toward me into a headwind. He spirals down until he hovers in space with wings outstretched, riding the *flow* as a union of awareness, will, and trust, emerging effortlessly from the flow with a simple demonstration of the harmony of these three actions. There is nothing for me to interpret or assign meaning

Medicine of One

to. The meaning is right there ~ in the moment.

A bee lands on my hand and seems to be gathering pollen from the flower formed by my open hand and spreading fingers. I turn my hand over as the bee continues its search on the backside. The palm of my hand stares back at me prevalent with the signs of my soul's journey. The lifeline breaks in the middle of my palm and leaps into a new path in the middle. I study the back where the bee is tracing the many scars darkened by the rays of the sun. My little finger bends inward from having been slammed in a car door as a boy. This wondrous form of the human hand, which artists draw because of its great complexity, has touched many thousands of people with the intent of liberation and peace for them. This hand was on the steering wheel of that Austin Healy I flipped, and has a trail of truth with its fingerprints, perhaps still present, from my very beginnings on a small tricycle now cycling in antique shops ... to the many wooden flutes I have played. A toy and a flute, play and creativity are the words that come from the bubble the bee brought into my Circle.

In many of the cliff dwellings and thousands of rock art sites in the Southwest, you will see the human hand gracing cliff walls with the presence of the Ancient Ones whom archaeologists call the Anasazi and the Hopi call *Hisatsinom*. In the mortar placed between the rocks, which form the dwelling walls, you will see ancient fingerprints. I have even seen the imprint of the small hand of a child pressed into the once soft cool mortar. These hands of creativity link me to a squirrel nibbling a berry that had to be creative in order to pluck it from a bush five feet off the ground. My hand links me to gorillas still surviving in the mountain forests of Africa and to the lizard sunning itself in my Circle.

I reach for a stick and hold it first as if it were a drumstick ready to tap the elk skin of a drum and release the rhythmic origins of music through its resonant sound. I grasp it delicately as if it were the handle of a paintbrush created by wrapping short strands of my own hair like Neanderthal man may have done when painting the cave walls of Lascaux. And finally, I lift the stick to my mouth with the ten tips of my fingers as if holding a flute birthing musical notes through my

Creativity is Married to the Spiritual Quest

own primal breath. There are so many different ways in which a hand engages the world and gives expression to the creative force of life. The index finger and the thumb join together in many actions as subtle as holding a pencil or a paintbrush. The human hand is capable of the power and artistry of a championship boxer or the powerful grip of a *Hall of Fame* baseball player, as he stands ready with his wooden bat to hit another home run. And yet, on the *other hand,* it is capable of the gentle slight movements of an artist drawing a human eye or the watchmaker's graceful placement of an infinitesimally small wheel in a watch that will mark the passage of time. Think of Mozart, Beethoven, Leonardo Da Vinci, Ernest Hemingway ... and our ancient ancestors creating the first tools, discovering the use of plants, painting and carving on the rocks, and giving form to the invisible. The human experience is endlessly creative, and the human hand is essential to so much of it and a great metaphor for the movement from *being* to creative *doing.* This *beingness* listens, sees, and expresses through actions of artful living and artistic creations that happen in this concrete world. Creativity can bring the two worlds of the visible and invisible into *one moment.*

My hands can also speak a language that is preverbal and closer to the symbolic language of the soul. The slightest articulation of the fingers, palm, and wrist convey many messages such as in a gesture of peace and love when I approach you and place my hand over my heart. It's a silent language communicating inner feeling that can reflect a full-bodied truth words cannot touch. There is great beauty and truth in our hands.

The raven reminded me to *be fully present* as the space of the Circle ... as the center. The bee delivered the bubble in response to my *quiet waiting* for the answer, and my hand reached out and spoke to me and I listened. What my hand speaks, in this moment, is that in the quest for what is ultimate truth, the Great Mystery comes forth from within through the play of the mind's creativity.

Part of the great wonder of human history and experience is creativity and art and its quest to express the seemingly inexpressible through the vibrational languages of song, poetry, dance, painting, sculpture, music, and all forms of creative expression through the manifestation of each person's unique spine of their life. People often believe because they are not an artist, they are not creative. But the very origins of humanity sprung from an innate creativity. Creative expression can be anything from cooking to teaching, from the politics of world peace to finding ways to help the poor and starving. To be human is to be creative; and the quest for truth and what is real is a creative journey.

Creativity is married to the spiritual quest. At some point we wake up like a chick cracking its shell, thrust our head into the real world and begin our creative quest. It's creative because we look beyond what is known and accepted as normal. Creativity is the mind breaking free of belief, exploring the unknown and honing in on that "true north." Imagine the first pioneers of this land creatively overcoming what seemed like insurmountable obstacles, driven by a passion for a new world. In the spiritual quest the new world is the true world.

It was a broken heart that cracked the egg where my creativity laid waiting. When we are young and in love, that love is the world. There is never another love quite like the first all consuming one. In the desolation of losing my world, it was as if *my hand* reached out through the shell wanting to express my suffering. From this loss my hand reached to the stars for the meaning in life through painting, writing, music, and acting. But it also reached for the truth that would lead me on my own creative journey to the center of the labyrinth.

In the fall of 1970 I chose to leave an expensive private school and head west to UC Berkley. I was majoring in English and Philosophy, but after one semester I decided I wanted to focus on writing, pottery making, and theater. I could not get into any of these classes so I quit and moved to San Francisco. There in my studio apartment, I painted a mural of *The Prodigal Son*. It was a self-portrait of breaking free of what I had unconsciously accepted as the practical path of my life: education should lead to the stability of earning an income. This was the beginning of my *coming home to my Self*. The birthing of my artistic expression and creativity evolved side by side with my spiritual quest. The creative force served that quest. My writ-

Creativity is Married to the Spiritual Quest

ing, my painting, my singing, and songs were full of the underside of life trying to come up out of the depths and speak.

I eventually worked tending bar in North Beach, San Francisco in bars that had been the roosting places for the likes of Allen Ginsberg and Jack Kerouac. I tended to poets, writers, painters, strippers, and old men living out their final years in the hotel rooms above the bars. One of the bars where I communed with these creative geniuses was called Vesuvio's. Mount Vesuvius is a stratovolcano on the west coast of Italy and is best known for its eruption in A.D. 79, which destroyed the city of Pompeii. A stratovolcano can erupt violently like a bottle of shaken soda. It is considered to be one of the most dangerous, life threatening volcanoes in the world due to the large population of Naples and the other surrounding towns on the slopes nearby. What a perfect name for the explosion of the Beat Poetry Era.

The word *beat* was primarily in use after World War II by jazz musicians and hustlers as a slang term meaning down and out, or poor and exhausted. Kerouac went on to twist the meaning of the term *beat* to serve his own purposes, explaining that it meant *beatitude*, not *beat up*. The *beat* of his writing followed the rhythm of what became known as *stream of consciousness* ... letting words emerge from the flow without the rules of what is acceptable or correct. It is listening to the beautiful beat of your own truthful drumming as a rhythm that comes forth from the flow and leads you forward.

I remember a famous poet left over from the beat poet era named Bobby Kaufman. He would wander up and down the aisle behind the bar stools muttering to himself. Every now and then he would pause at the bar and sip his pint of beer. It was said his condition was the result of electroshock treatments. Sometimes it's the designated insane that are the most enlightened. They don't speak the same linear language that moves straight through time but in a *spatial language of the timeless.* In many cultures these people are often known as the *see-ers* of the less visible world and have now commonly been given the name *shaman*. They tread the line between the visible and the invisible world and in doing so help people break free of their hardened identity, which is rooted in the visible,

Medicine of One

material world. They are artists who creatively merge these worlds and inspire those whose lives they touch to walk the fine line ~ the flow where these worlds are not separate. This walking is a creative dance.

Another drinking establishment I worked at was called The Saloon, whose swinging doors were left over from a movie filmed there. Right down the street from the Saloon was the Coffee Gallery, which had hosted Janis Joplin in the early 60's. I signed up weekly on open mike night and played my guitar and sang. I was writing songs, poetry, and working on a novel while observing life and the suffering of the human heart. And I was drinking, reveling, and creating in the artistic underworld of North Beach, San Francisco, side by side with poets, painters, and a plethora of hippies, flower children, and the *down and out*. North Beach, San Francisco was the beginning of my decent into the underworld. It was as if all the creative and suffering souls gathered for an endless party of drinking and reveling. I danced with them for a few years but I knew I couldn't stay there too long, or I would fall into the drug induced sleep and limbo of Dante's Divine Comedy. There was a poem I penned 40 years ago at the age of twenty-three as if calling out to a power and presence within us, myself included, to awaken. As I read it now I can see the vestiges of the Medicine of One. Here are just a few lines.

> Remember, Oh remember
> We are all torchbearers, light bringers...
>
> Hearts were meant to be filled, not emptied
> Laughter was meant to reveal joy, not to cover
>   your pain...
>
> So many fallen birds that have forgotten
> Once in wide open spaces you could sing ....
>
> Oh Isis, come find our parts
> Come make us whole again
> So like new life we might rise up
> And grab the fleecy white belly of sheep

Creativity is Married to the Spiritual Quest

> And ride out of towns with
> our hearts and minds ...

A few years later I began to train as an actor with the same intent as the young man who read Henry David Thoreau's *Walden* and was inspired to become a writer ~ to know the human heart and to awaken through the search and exploration of humanity. It had to be an experiential exploration not from the point of view of a psychologist, which is from the outside in through labels and analysis, but from the inside out ... to know what drives behavior from within my own heart.

I kept journals because I knew one day I would teach. The question for me as an actor was what made the best actor? What I discovered was that the true geniuses of theater and film who I admired were able to believe in an imaginary story, and through their character's behavior they were able to be completely in the moment with their fellow actors, the atmosphere of the scene, and the stage set of the imaginary environment. Their creativity sprang from the power of *now* where the magic happens. This meant that the controlling mind had to somehow be "parked" so inspired creativity could flow through. At that time I made this my goal.

The marriage of creativity to the spiritual quest is in part about allowing our behavior to spring from the truth of who we are, not from *how* we will be *seen* and *judged* by others. This is authenticity. For the actor the stakes of wanting to be loved and appreciated are heightened. The challenge is how to get the controlling mind out of the way so spontaneity can happen. Creativity and spontaneity are synonymous. Creativity flows from the *now* and when we surrender to creativity it delivers us into the *now*. When you are living in the moment, fully present and responding from that presence, you are open and compassionate and able to meet life creatively, free of the old scripts. You are not in the past or the future worrying ... you are in the now of the flow. But when the old stories of the past create an imaginary now that you are reacting to, you are aligning yourself with a character formed by rejected pain and unmoved emotions who believes this world they *think* they are seeing is the real world. But it's no different than the actor's imaginary world and from this ... drama ensues.

My initial training was very unconventional. It harkened back to Beck's Living Theater and Grotowski's explorations of unbridled expressiveness. It was visceral and soulful, using the whole range of body movement and voice, and cultivated complete unrestricted spontaneity. This unbridled body and voice training allowed me to eventually create and develop what I call "primordial movements." These are very specific psychological postures joined with words that are part of a *story* spoken in emotional tones. They immediately invoke complicated "feeling states." This training was followed by what are known as "sense memory" and "emotional memory," which is training your body and emotions to respond to an *imaginary now.* These exercises were fundamental to what became known as "Method Acting" in the 1950's. Some of the actors who emerged from this method were Marlon Brando, James Dean, Montgomery Cliff, and Marilyn Monroe. This kind of training led me into something called "Transformational Acting," which took these exercises a step further by using the imagination in unique ways to generate authentic feeling.

At that time I had no idea what these skills were *really* training me for. Fifteen years later in 1990, when putting my hands on a friend to do energy healing, *Soul Dreaming* spontaneously came forth. I grabbed the thread of a soul story and lived it for that person encouraging them to feel it with me. The training of my voice as a singer and speaker allowed me to transmit the full range of feeling from a whisper to a scream. It was all of this training that allowed me to use the human body to invoke authentic feeling for others. But it was also a tool for myself that served my own personal spiritual quest, because central to my ability to do this is the ability to be in the *unobstructed now*.

My quest took me back and forth across the continent from San Francisco to New York City and back to the West Coast in Los Angeles. This was my own personal migration in the four directions. At some point I was ready for the desert and ready for the home that would draw forth my own spine of this life. These migrations were full of artistic creativity, yes,

Creativity is Married to the Spiritual Quest

but the journey itself was mapped by a creativity that was invoked to arrive at this *home*. The truth within us is a living thing that creatively seeks to come forth.

All of my creative explorations and experience, all of my skills and talents, came together when *I was in the desert and the desert was in me. Coming home to this land* became the missing piece of the puzzle for me that mobilized and aligned all of my talents into a single thrust. Writing the *Medicine of One* was part of a creative journey that was aligned with my own personal quest. This is how I live and this is how I work with people. Each day we enter the unknown together and share in a creative *clearing the way to home*. This is when the magic happens.

Creativity happens in the moment of *now* and that now is the destination of the spiritual quest. Every single one of us is naturally creative. It doesn't matter what you do. If you are a master at solving computer problems, you are focused and your creativity is finding a solution that helps someone be at peace. If you are a teacher and you want to find a way to help students learn difficult ideas of science and physics, how you do that is creative and it's fueled by an impulse to inspire the desire to learn and explore. This creative presence is the spine of your life. No matter what you do the thrust of the spine of your life is there. It has always been there, but sometimes it has to wait for us to wake up to its truth. It is like an agave that shoots a stalk up when the moment is ripe. This primary thrust of your presence, this spine, may have appeared in sundry ways throughout your life but was undermined and derailed by living from a place of survival and fear. You were then unable to get out of the way and allow it to be enlivened and aligned with the flow of the Great Mystery.

Let life flow through this spine of your life and carry you home to yourself in the immediacy of the moment. Let it deliver you to what was never farther than your own heartbeat. Creativity brings us into the *moment of the Self.* It can both free and invoke the soul. It is living in the moment and letting life spontaneously move through you *in* the flow and *as* the flow. It doesn't know. When you embrace *I don't know* ~ you embrace creativity. As creativity flows forth from us, it carries us into the deeper flow of life and connects us with the creative force of the universe and beyond. This creative force is a great ally in the journey to peace. It's a dance of invention and imagination, a child's original innocence of play and joy. Free yourself and play. Celebrate your humanity in the delicate balance between the wisdom of innocence and the wisdom of experience that are freed from the stories of pain. Balanced innocence has no pretention of knowing and lives in the immediate moment of a child's wonder. Experience knows all, but when joined with innocence it embraces the experience of magic and intuition.

Let your creativity be free of the need to be understood, appreciated, valued, and even seen, by allowing its true purity of the movement from the flow. Let it be free of this need by being the compassionate Circle to the need. Sing even if you are off key. Paint if it helps you discover what needs to move inside of you. Write a poem about a moment in life you want to value. Value your *Self*! Share your *Self*. Give and receive. If you are reading this book let it be the beginning or a continuance of walking a path. If you walk the path, your value and true power of *beingness* will come up from the depths within you, where it lies waiting for the light of your own loving eyes. No matter who you are or what you do your own truth is waiting for you to creatively come home. Imagination is not equal to illusion if it's used as a guide to walking the path to your truth. Imaginative thoughts can lead to truth when they are free of fear, worry, desire, and the need to control.

It is as simple as the raven hovering motionless in being, but with true doing. In the creative journey of the quest, prayer, surrender, faith, flow, and magic all come together in the *Great Compassionate Mystery that is you* when they are united through the marriage of awareness, will, and trust. This is a marriage made possible by the union of creativity and the innate impulse within all of us to come *Home.*

Part Four
CHOICE

Medicine of One

"Can you give me some kind of herb or plant to stop my thinking so that I can see this truth?"

"This is not my way. My way is perhaps slower, but more permanent."

Singing Deer took a great breath and sighed out with deep resignation. He opened his mouth to say something but stopped himself after the first word. "I ... "

"Good. Weigh this choice as something you will serve," Lomakayu said softly. "Take your time."

"I choose ... " He looked over at the dogs as if they sat there quietly speaking the only choice. "I choose your way. I choose the truth of peace."

"Choose truth and how that way comes through the wisdom within. You can't choose somebody else's way."

"I am confused. You offer your way to me and then you say I can't choose it."

"I share my path but then you must walk it, and test it, and practice it, and let the truth come to you through your own knowing. That could be a path that is very much like my own and you can use the name that I have given it, the Medicine of One, the Path of the Circle. But still, you must walk it to make it your own."

From *The Circle of Life*
Lomakayu

Chapter Twenty-One

Choosing Harmlessness or Greed

*An open hand is like an open heart both offering
and capable of receiving. A tight fist can both
grasp, and be used as a weapon with
which to strike and take what it wants.*

The Hopi believe we live in the fourth world and are moving into the fifth. Each world prior to this was destroyed by cataclysms, the last one being a flood. But the truth of what really destroyed each world was greed. We can be greedy for many things: power, land, resources, love, money or anything you want, desire or think will give you value, safety, power, and ultimately control. Here we meet our friend again ~ control driven by fear.

Greed in the sense the Hopi speak of is not necessarily evil. It is serving the little **i** rather than the greater *we* of the world. When I say *the world*, I mean something more than a group, tribe, or single nation. There are many tribes who feel this responsibility to keep the whole world in balance. They do not function from the mindset of tribalism. But tribalism has been a ruling force on this planet since people joined together in bands, which evolved into tribes and shared beliefs that differed from other tribes. Each tribe believes they are right and have a right of ownership to resources and land. Tribes can grow into religions, countries, and even institutions that all serve the little **i,** where the head is separated from the heart. It's all about separation and power.

Medicine of One

Greed. Even the word has a hard, stiff, stubborn resolve to hold on and grab more. Greed can seem cruel and violent in its drive to acquire what it wants or what it thinks it needs. Or it can be ignorant to the needs of others, never pausing to consider the harm it is doing. Greed causes harm. One of the expressions in the world of the Medicine of One is *harmlessness*. So if harm comes from serving the little **i**, it makes sense that liberating that little **i** from the pain and beliefs that obscure its *compassionate seeing* is a worthy path for world peace.

If four entities called Greed, Fear, Love, and Harmlessness enter a room famished and hungry, almost starving to death, and they sit down at a table with a great feast before them, what would happen? Greed is likely to grab everything at once and own it all because it's not only thinking about the moment, but also its *future needs.* Greed is the little **i** whose world is as small as the little spinning dot on top of that vertical line. It lives in a very small world preoccupied with its own needs. It is driven by survival beyond what it needs in the moment, because it is thinking of the future and it remembers the past pain of hunger. Food on a table is a metaphor for anything that could be *desired.* This kind of greed is driven by great fear.

Fear is caught in the middle. It wants to grab a big portion for itself for fear of dying from hunger but it fears the aggressive Greedy one as a force that could harm or hurt it. So Fear feels paralyzed and powerless. Greed has been empowered by possession, a false power, since true power can neither be taken away nor bartered for.

Love sits quietly waiting with Harmlessness, but in essence they are sisters of the same mother of peace. Their peace is who they are. They know this. They are at peace with death and they are at peace with life. They will let the flow decide the outcome and surrender to the great mystery of that flow. They will exude their calm deep presence of Harmlessness and Love that it may resonate into the hearts of Fear and Greed. Harmlessness and Love are not out of balance and are not afraid to ask for a fair portion. Their *passiveness* must not be mistaken for Fear. They are, in fact, infused with the great-

Choosing Harmlessness or Greed

est courage ~ the courage to be the big I that unites heaven and sky, and do not hold their wanting as more important than anyone else's needs. This is the courage of Nelson Mandela, Chief Joseph, Gandhi, Saint Francis, Christ, and Buddha.

They do not judge because they have loved and touched their own Fear and Greed within themselves. They do not stand above anyone. But they have chosen a path ~ a path that is self-love, a path that is Harmless in its actions, Harmless to themselves. Harmlessness, as this deep love and respect for life, radiates out into the world. They live at the center that is responsible for the whole world. They live at the center that is connected to all things, all humans. In this path they choose to serve the greater Circle, which their individual Circle is part of. They have been the spacious breathing Love to their own deep wanting ~ *to survive and to be loved.* They have loved their own *I want to be loved* and *feelings of powerlessness.* Or you could say they have surrendered their thinking and let the Circle heal them by aligning themselves with it. They sit as the center of the Circle of compassion, first for themselves and then for Fear and Greed. They wait and do not judge.

Greed can be driven by ignorance that is lacking awareness and compassion. The table could be laid out as a map of land to be owned. It has resources, people, and riches. Greed doesn't just want food. It wants power and control. The point is, excessive Greed can seem to those who are victimized by it as pure evil and cruelty, as a demonic exercise of power over others.

Greed has countless forms, which bring the world out of balance. It's easy to see the Greed in the Wall Street scams of our day and in people who have plundered and conquered others throughout human history. I could find endless examples of this but it's important to look at the lesser forms that Greed can take. A farmer could be greedy with his land by farming it until it is without life and nutrients. He can take and take from the land to make more money to the point where he has defeated himself and harmed the land. He has been harmful by living from scarcity and Greed. He has allowed Fear to own him. If you have a strong judgment against the Greedy and selfish, look for Greed in yourself, rather than pointing your finger at others. It may be within you, hidden in some disguised form.

Greed occurs when someone is trying to gain something to make them feel powerful, whole, valuable, and safe, something from the outside involving a relationship with someone or something else. It is driven by the core, dark feeling of powerlessness. Greed has no path but the straight path to getting what it wants. Harmlessness sees equality and puts itself in the shoes of others, as the *Golden Rule* in many religions states, "Do unto others as you would have them do unto you." Blaming others for what you feel because you don't get what you want, clinging righteously to your opinion, hanging on tightly to all or any of your stories, can empower Greed to rule you from the underworld.

There is no positive in this word Greed. That's why it is not the same as selfishness. Sometimes selfishness is healthy when it is a true act of self-love. It's healthy for someone who has always sacrificed their sense of self to others by always saying "Yes," to say "No." But others can see this as selfish. Fulfilling the emotional needs of others, feeding their *hungry ghosts,* so to speak, to avoid their disapproval and judgment can be *self-obliterating.*

You may be a naturally generous person, but the great generosity of the *One* should channel effortlessly through you, gifting you and the world. Those who are connected to the great mystery, able to surrender to how it expresses itself through them with trust and awareness filtered through their own unique genius, are not burdened by too much giving that makes them weary and tired. Their experience is not one of sacrifice. They have moved from the little **i** to the big **I** and beyond.

The unintegrated sources of Fear and desire drive us to live from the spins in the Circle that cry for abundance from the feeling of lack ~ lack of love, value, power, and safety. To bring them into the Circle and hold them as a mother holds a child, holding the deep *fragileness* within, is the movement back to the center, back to the place of living Harmlessly both to yourself and to others. My message is to live at the *center of the Circle* of who you are and let that be your gift to the world

Choosing Harmlessness or Greed

as a natural and effortless generosity, the same easy generosity as a flower's scent draws the bees and gifts the air for us to enjoy. This is *living at the center of the Circle of who you are.*

Choose the path that is the *true action of self-love* to arrive there. This true action of self-love grows into a true love and respect for the earth and humanity. Don't spend time trying to fix the world with your will. This willfulness can be driven by your own need for value. Choose the path that serves the whole without projecting a righteous judgment that demands others to change so it can have peace. *Be the demonstration* of how you want the world to behave. Live the path without needing *others* to live it. Live the integrated forces of trust, awareness, creative will, and compassion.

Medicine of One

Chapter Twenty-Two

To Be the Circle

*To be the Circle is a journey to the truth of who
you are as you clear the way to your deep listening,
and enter the flow that carries you home.*

There is a Circle by the river ... a very special Circle. It is partially *encircled* by sheer cliff walls of volcanic rock rising up around it in the form of rock beings. The whole canyon through which the river flows appears as if pillared by these rock beings. I call this the Canyon of the Holy Beings. They stand above you as witnesses to millions of years of flowing river. These rock beings are a constant presence within constant change. That presence is like your own *true* presence in the midst of constant change.

The predominant element of water visibly creates movement and flow. So I have christened this Circle, the Circle of Change. This is a Circle that visibly disappears, one, two, maybe three times a year. It can happen from the flooding river flowing furiously over it. Sometimes when the water recedes, the Circle is still there, *encircled* by a canal of water. Other times there is not a trace left, just a mound of bone white rocks.

This bone white rock comes from above and is not deposited by the river. There is a large wash in the cliffs above, which is several miles long and travels through an area called Skeleton Bone, which can bring a different kind of *disappearing act* to the Circle. The waters pour down during summer monsoons completely cleansing the whole area and depositing more bone white rock. This bone white rock is very special to me. I place it in all of my Circles. But only this Circle is *in* the bone rock, surrounded by the Holy Beings. And only this Circle frequently seems to disappear.

The power of the place is always there as a mysterious presence that is difficult to put into words. You can always feel this presence if you pause to step into the *flow*. Building the Circle in this place is honoring that power in one sense, but also gives the Circle a tangible feeling. Having a rock Circle around you is an aid of remembrance of who you are. You gift the Circle with your presence and it gifts you. But the Circle is both a symbol and an experience of your true compassionate self. Like this Circle I have described, that compassionate presence never goes away. It never disappears. It *can't*. We go away. We forget, and our feeling of connection seems to disappear. But our compassionate presence is always here waiting for us to remember.

The mind turned outward to the world is a Circle cluttered with duality. The mind turned inward toward itself is the quiet compassionate Circle. It is the one sea of truth upon which the duality dances. The mind turned inward to the little i is the big I, the self. *To be the Circle is a journey to the truth of who you are as you clear the way to your deep listening, and enter the flow that carries you home.*

To be the Circle is to be who you are. How beautiful to live in the world being who you truly are! *To be the Circle* means to expand with your very breath as a life-giving God of your world and then to expand with the mind beyond the very breadth of who *you think* you are. It means to give up being anchored in believing your thinking and *be* the loving space in which everything moves. And in this spacious, all-encompassing detachment, *to be the Circle* is to penetrate beneath the apparent surface spins of thinking to rejected emotional forces that are driving the thoughts to free the energy, and to let all things within you move in the presence of peace. It is a medicine without the intent to medicate, fix, change, cure, or even heal. It is the liberation of your radiance.

You as the Circle are timeless. Being caught up in the spins and movements in the Circle, the surface movement, is

To Be the Circle

living in time, a prisoner of time. If you use the means of time to try to free yourself you weave an inextricable web. If you use psychological analysis and mental understanding to liberate yourself, you are just swimming around in your stories and you liberate nothing. You keep exercising the mind as an outward directed force probing the objects of your past, your stories. You strengthen the one who wants to be in control. *If I know why I do what I do, I will be able to control it.* Thinking is the lock, and unmoved emotions from these stories are the substance of the closed door.

You must root yourself in the timeless, but in order to do this you must penetrate to the *emotional charges that are rooting you in time,* and liberate them with the loving breath of the Circle. Our *soul's history* is as if imprinted in a field of memory. Archetypes can be stories we resonate with. We carry imprints that are like a vibrational pattern, a resonance that seeks to reenact the same story over and over again. This penetrates us on every level, emotionally, mentally and physically. We are driven by these energetic stories and imprints of what has come before, and they drive us from the underworld where all we have abandoned, rejected, and thrown out of the Circle crawls around in the dark waiting, waiting for the light of your loving, spacious awareness to liberate it. Examination, analysis, even understanding will not liberate us from these stories. Liberation comes from gathering these emotional energies back into the Circle of your love.

To be the Circle is to allow the trapped and rejected emotional life of the soul to vibrate and sing with the lost notes of your music to free you from the story, to free you from its thinking. You bring rejected emotional experience back into the Circle of life with your very *life giving breath* which gives it permission to move and speak its truth in tone, in movement, as vibration. You cease believing in your story. This is *To be the Circle.*

To be the Circle for another is no different than being the Circle for yourself. How could it be different? *To be the Circle* for another is to be the deep listening, *I am here* presence for them. *To be the Circle* is to be who you are. And *To be the Circle* for another is to be who you are.

Medicine of One

You can't *be the Circle* to another if you are thinking and trying to be right. If the need to be right is ruling the quality of your presence then it's a good place to come face to face with your own righteousness. If you can't be the quiet compassionate Circle for another and find yourself defending, attacking, justifying, and fortifying your position turn your compassionate awareness to what is being threatened within you and to the host of feelings that are moving. What we have separated from inside of ourselves through rejection and thinking are the same actions that separate us from others. The *way home*, out of feeling alone and isolated, is the compassionate Circle for yourself, which radiates out effortlessly to others.

To be the Circle is to love your own imperfections and your reactions to others' behavior. Your reactions are generated by how you perceive behavior, which is based on a worldview ... a lens created by your unintegrated history. Why not choose to enter all your relationships with this compassion and free yourself from your history? You must begin with the true action of self-love for yourself. Without compassion for yourself, compassion for others is manufactured because compassion is who you are.

You cannot willfully *try to be the Circle*. The Circle as compassion is not something that you *do*. You don't think compassion or manufacture the energy in response to a counter feeling. Willfully trying to be compassion just creates another spin in the Circle. While one part hates and dislikes what you are feeling, another part is compassionate to it. This is separation. *To be the Circle* and the true action of self-love is being your quiet presence, which is compassion and peace ... you are not trying to feel or think compassion. Your quiet presence *is* compassion.

The Circle has many levels of meaning and experience. It begins as a way to describe the energetics of life force, the connected consciousness of life; of *you* in its original unobstructed presence as an open heart, like the radiance of the *sun of who you are*. At times it's a metaphorical form, which allows us to talk about something that is ultimately formless and nameless. How else can we learn? How else can we teach?

To Be the Circle

How else can we share the wisdom of experience? In the beginning these words and tools are necessary so we can understand the path, so we can give our earnest commitment. We take care of the mind's need to know and understand, and honor that so we can use that same mind to help us surrender to what we now have clarity about. In that surrender we give up all the words, the concepts, the thoughts, the metaphors, and the doing ~ so we can walk the path.

The Circle is a place you go *to,* to reinforce this sense. It is a choice to sit in the truth. You sit there as a spacious, relaxed, breathing presence that allows the opposites to be there simultaneously. You sit there to touch, to free, and to be compassionate to the prisoner energies of fear, terror, rage, sadness, and the unlimited mix of these ingredients, both lived and unlived, in the stories of your soul. You allow them to tremble through your body as a coldness, as a warmth, as a quivering lip, as a sudden tightness, as a tear forming like a dew drop or erupting into sobbing, as laughter, as thinking that won't stop, but continuing to be spacious to all the sensations of life moving.

To be the Circle is to be uninvolved in your thinking. You practice being the quiet to all the noise without judgment as to success or failure. Just honor yourself for the choice to take this time away from the *time* that daily owns you. Slowly being the Quiet One, the Circle becomes easier. When you become too busy and are drawn out of the center you will miss the *peaceful quiet being.* You will wish to dwell in this quiet and be the Circle even when there are no challenges or disturbances. It will become your *first nature.*

This is the *true action of self-love* and this is *clearing the way* ~ clearing the way to the truth of *you.* So, at the same time, this Circle is you in an openhearted state, but you can also have a physical Circle on the land that is your church upon the earth and beneath the sky. It's a place where it's easy just to be. This sacred earth is a constant demonstration of this presence of self. There are limitless *gurus of nature* waiting to help you just by the song of their presence, and in that *presence* guide you with their resonance home to the *guru within,* your own presence.

Medicine of One

The wondrous world of natural power and glory is an aid, a tool, to help direct *you* back into yourself. The doorway to this absolute truth is closer than you think. There is nothing more immediate and undeniable than the experience that you are. You are here. Beyond that, the truth gets watered down with ideas and concept.

This book is not about tools or step-by-step methods to instruct you how to *clear the way*. There are countless methods out there that can help with that. There are countless books out there that dissect the anatomy of human existence. I have stayed away from these concepts and this language because I have it found unnecessary. I have shared some of the tools of my work that I use with my clients and myself. I have found these tools after many years of letting them reveal themselves to be effortless and almost spontaneous if one can surrender the controlling mind. But the essence of the Medicine of One is not about these tools. It's about your presence as a quiet compassionate *hereness* that I call **The Circle.** The Medicine of One is about rooting yourself in this presence as you journey through life, the good times and the bad times. It's about knowing what *the true action of self-love* is and how that can bring you peace even in those difficult times. In that sense there is no tool or technique. Breath, relaxation, and awareness are not techniques or tools. They are life itself. They are how you want to move through life all the time.

I am asking you to reverse a lifetime habit. I am asking you to reenter the feeling body and feel without labeling, feel without knowing why, feel without intent ... just feel. But feel as a spaciousness that allows the energy to be in motion, as opposed to the thinking that would hold, freeze, control, and manipulate the motion.

Wherever you are, whatever the situation, draw a Circle around yourself with your finger in the dirt or the dust or with your very mind and sit in the form of your own sacred presence. Sit there and find out what the presence is beneath, beyond, and at the source of all the thinking. Touch this with your attention until your attention abides in it even if only for a few seconds. Even if you are confined to a bed because of an illness, the Circle is always there. Fill the space all around your

To Be the Circle

presence and let that expanded presence establish the bed as the ground of your Circle. Let that bed become the gentle warm hand that is your greater presence to your fear, to your anger, to whatever emotional energy is moving within you. And if everything is okay then be the quiet. Let this be a sacred time.

There are many paths home to the truth of who you are, but this *home* is One and the same. If the Medicine of One sits right with you and the world you wish to move in, drink it gently. Drink the quiet, fill with it, and melt into this ocean of One. Be the Circle. Clear the way and be who you are.

Medicine of One

Chapter Twenty-Three

The Path
*Be the demonstration of how you want the world to behave.
Live the path without needing others to live it.*

I embrace the Medicine of One as a *path* woven into the fabric of my life. All of my actions are infused with it. This doesn't mean I am faultless or perfect. It means I have compassion for my faults and imperfections, rather than ceaseless judgment and self-criticism. I learn from my mistakes without suffering beneath the label of failure. There is no *idea* of perfection, success, or failure. There is no image of something I am trying to show the world. There is only living and walking the path. Every day is different. Every day I am different. It's a commitment to *be* the Circle and live at the center of the Circle, harmless, compassionate, and free of history.

The impulse to live this path is from within. It's a choice to live as something greater than your stories. A compassion that begins with yourself and sees through that which obstructs your vision and prevents you from knowing *home* has always been right where you stand in this world. This allows you to move toward the center of that Circle of who you are, your deepest, truest, most absolute self, so that you can extend that compassion effortlessly into the world. This becomes your gift to the world in all its uniqueness filtered through the balance and harmony of your human form. Right where you are now, in this moment, as you read these words ... quietly feel the path that is within you. Walking the path frees the flow of the spine of your life. No matter what the spine of

Medicine of One

your life is, it invokes *deep compassionate listening*, the essence of your presence. There is no other way. That's how you live in the flow and allow it to flow through you and through the spine of your life. The path allows you to remain aligned with this spine. They are inseparable. Your spine is part of the path. That is why the phrase that embodies the spine of your life usually begins with the words "to be." Living the spine of your life is the path of presence: your full, complete *hereness in the world.* You are serving something greater than the spins in your Circle. This service is done through you, not by you. *Deep compassionate listening* is not tied to your identity because this power of your presence transcends your personal identity. The spine of your life is the simplest expression of your path. It demands your compassionate presence no matter what it is.

To Be the Circle of compassion is how you move to the center of the Circle. *Living at the center* is a great commitment to the greater good of all without having an idea, a concept, or mission. In each moment, you keep choosing to live from a place of compassion and harmlessness, whether you are in a hurry driving through traffic or standing behind someone at the grocery store who's cashing in dozens of coupons.

You walk the path by learning what the *true action of self-love* is. Reading this book is not walking the path. Your analytical mind can give you understanding, but you must use your mind as a deep compassionate *listening* to walk it. You start with the small Circle of the **i** and you give your compassionate attention to this and all the spins of that little dot of your *personality* that creates separation through its endless stories and thinking. You begin to taste and feel that this attentive, witnessing awareness without judgment is closer to who you really are than that little **i** is. And you keep cultivating that sense of this greater *you* as if moving into larger and larger Circles with less and less definition.

This path has been a living thing that has grown over a half of a century of my life and twenty years of helping others live in their truth. In the last two decades, I can say with clear honesty it has allowed me to have peace and to continue to enjoy my *love of being,* while continuing to keep rooting myself each day in something greater that can only be described as

The Path

the great mystery. It is in this honoring, I share what has allowed me to give into the *flow* of this mystery and to never give up even in my darkest days, weeks, months, and years.

There was a period when everything failed that had previously worked. I sought help in every direction available. Physically, everything was collapsing and pressuring my brain stem, sending intense distress into my autonomic nervous system. After a routine of sauna to warm my body, Qigong to open my head and neck, and yoga to balance everything, my plan would be to go sit in the Circle and be quiet. But often I would have to lie back down by noon. Work seemed impossible but I let my *warrior* push me out of bed and go through the motions lest I give in to my *victim*. I tried to walk a path of balance between the two, neither pushing too hard, nor giving in to hopeless thoughts. Everything was disappearing: my work and livelihood, the places and stillness I loved, and exercise. I lived in a constant state of exhaustion barely able to climb out of bed. There were days on end of constant vertigo and exhaustion ... and a feeling of absence. My mind was gone ... it seemed. So I lay in bed one morning wondering, *How can I walk this path without the clear attention of my mind, without moving about and living it?* There was only one answer. I had to be compassionate to this frailty lying in bed, unable to think, unable to move, and almost unable, it seemed, to be a *compassionate presence*.

How could I walk a path of neither pushing nor sinking into worry, both of which invoke tension? Tension is the opposite of this compassion. How could I not react with a survivalist's tension when the world was tumbling down around me? Absence and frailty were death and death was now my teacher. I could struggle with my feelings of powerlessness or I could lovingly hold these feelings in my arms and invoke freedom through my compassion.

Even though I felt absent, and without the power and focus of my mind, something within me was aware of this. Something was present as the Circle in which it all was happening. So now this path demanded that I abide in it, that I align with it, and in that aligning serve the spine of my life, which is *To be Peace*. Once again, I chose to serve the spine of

Medicine of One

my life as my path, which is the *Medicine of One*. What will you do?

It is a life path that never ends. But as long as you are walking it ... living it ... this is all that counts. With your desire to align with the Truth of Self, coupled with the determination to leap out of the grooves, your arrival at the center becomes inevitable, an inevitability that must be allowed to happen without trying to control the timetable. This is why treating this walk to the center and living the spine of your life as *a path* is important, because it helps free you of time.

Live this path and the balance and harmony return. Awareness is cultivated to outweigh ignorance. Trust is allowed as you free yourself from the stories that seem to steal it from you. Trust brings the analytical mind of control into service to the Circle as a force that can serve the center, rather than the greed for your own survival only, which we do from ignorance. Fear drives the imbalance. The path is meeting your fear as compassionate presence. Be the demonstration of how you want the world to behave. Live the path without needing others to live it. Live the integrated forces of trust, awareness, creative will, and compassion.

As long as we live, we are in movement. Perhaps upon arrival at this center we have learned the skill of how to stay in balance and harmony in an ever-changing world. Walking the path is its own homecoming and reclamation of your power and energetic being, which senses the wind like a ready sail, and aligns its power to the wind of the great mystery. It is a *knowing* and a trust that guides you with a kind of instinct. So as long as we are here, moving and inhabiting this home of flesh and bones, the journey continues ... energized from within by your *path*.

Chapter Twenty-Four

Earnest Commitment

*Know what you want ~ peace.
Understand the path ~ presence.
Honor your uniqueness ~ spine of your life.
Align it with your chosen path ~ be the demonstration.*

One night long ago, as a very young man, I gazed up into the night sky. It was as if somehow, laid out in the pattern of the stars, there was a silent message that brought me into the feeling of my purpose for being here on earth. There was no clear message, no mission delineated, no importance bestowed upon me. It was as if an unnamable *flame of desire to awaken* took ahold of me. From then on no matter what I did this flame drove it. Whether it was my writing, acting, theater, being a merchant marine, traveling through civil wars in Nicaragua, living alone in a redwood forest, or studying English and Philosophy at UC Berkeley, the flame was always there.

The quest had begun. To the onlooker it would not look like the ordinary quest for spiritual truth. My journey had to involve the underbelly of life. In the search for peace I had to swim in chaos. In reaching for the life of truth I had to die in many ways: face to face with the pavement beneath my Austin Healy; on my back with a knife at my throat in Colon, Panama; taking LSD laced with strychnine alone in the woods; and stumbling down the snowy streets of New York City after blowing flaming 151 rum out of my mouth. But the true flame could never die. It refused to be denied its presence.

For many years I also read voraciously from Plato to Sartre to Jean Genet's *Our Lady of the Flowers*, from books about prison escape like *Papillon*, to Lawrence Durrell's *Alexandria Quartet*, which explores experience from different points of view. I played the parts of old and young men in pain in the plays of Tennessee Williams, Sam Shepard, and Eugene O'Neil's *Long Day's Journey Into Night*. I had to know the underworld from the inside out and the outside in. I had to know the core that drives suffering.

To an onlooker of my early life, it may have looked as though I was wondering all over the place. But I was threading through the essence of this earthly life as a human, bead by bead. Without knowing it at the time these beads would eventually complete the Circle I would later commit myself to.

So that original flame, ignited beneath a starry sky, carried a silent, unspoken commitment to why I was here which persisted as a kind of undercurrent of destiny. Something within me was gathering skills and experience that would awaken into gifts that were part of my sacred uniqueness. Eventually, it was the ancient land of the Southwest that brought the wisdom of experience and my gifts all together, as the Medicine of One, whose thrust is anchored into *the spine of my life*. I had to quest, to question, to search, explore, and finally I had to *earnestly commit.*

Before you commit you explore and search. Something burns in you for the truth and reality. For some this begins as a child. No matter what happens in life, this desire is still the primary driving force. For others, even though the desire was there in the beginning, it gets lost in the shuffle. Then, as life changes, what once seemed important becomes meaningless. The deep desire for peace and truth comes to the surface from the depths of their being. In either case, the inspired action is *The Quest,* the search, the seeking. This is where the movement towards your *truth of self* begins.

From *The Quest* comes *questioning.* Questioning is the child of *The Quest.* Questioning on your path in order to understand and experience is good. There is so much that we

Earnest Commitment

habitually do in life without questioning.

Many of the great realized Ones invite and welcome the *questioners*. It is in the exchange of questioning and answering that real communication is ignited. When truth is being spoken, words ride on a vibrational wave of rhythm, tones, and intent. The *presence* of the speaker is what makes the words vibrate with truth, but it is the *question from the seeker* that invokes the speaker's flow. But the *quest* is the deeper movement that sets in motion the circle of communication.

The written word can also have this vibration when you actually read at a slow enough speed to engage the music of its tone, rhythm, and intent. When you ride the wave of meaning and truth, you have entered an exchange with the author. You have moved beyond the quest for information into the poetics of the flow from where the author is speaking ... if you are not in the rule of your clever intellect.

Questioning this Medicine of One is good until you understand and either agree or disagree. Question, explore, probe, seek ... but at some point you must surrender the intellectual quest and relax into the arms of trust. You must believe from the deep listening that you have found a path to enter the flow and give yourself to it. You believe what is said, you understand what is to be done, even though you haven't arrived at the experience. Your intellect will not deliver you to the experience. This is where a great majority of people can detour for eternity. They keep *thinking* if they understand *it that* will be the key.

For many seeking the truth, finding an answer can go on endlessly as a person acquires more information and seeks out one teacher after another. They seek from the expectation of an experience. Their seeking is really no different than that of the hungry ghost. There is a wanting to be filled with something. They fasten onto an idea of enlightenment. It doesn't happen ... so they keep seeking one person, one book after another. The seeking that began in their heart is transferred to the mind.

They might be brilliant in their understanding of the *spiritual ideas* and the foundation of human existence. But a brilliant mind does not equal an *awakened mind.* Christ, the Buddha, and Ramana Maharshi were not philosophers in spite of the fact that they could dance circles around the philosophers of their time. And the reason they could do this is because they came from the *experience* of *One* not from the *concept* or *idea* of *One.*

To truly enter the flow where everything is *One,* you must earnestly commit. Even paths that say they aren't a path or a teaching cannot escape the action of commitment to them. *The Quest and questioning must one day lead to earnest commitment.* At some point you have to stop looking for another version of the answer to *Who am I* with your intellect, and commit yourself to *experiencing* the answer ... because you *are* the answer. There is no answer *outside* of you. And here we are again at *simple, but not easy. Just be quiet, abide in the awareness.*

Even all this understanding I am presenting to you is not *walking the path of the Circle.* You can have great intellectual understanding and, in fact, be brilliant in that understanding, but it's only more fortification. Reading books, chasing after gurus, shamans, saints, and all the forms in which wisdom comes to us in human form is not walking the path, whatever that path may be.

Even completely *getting it, understanding it* is not *walking* the path. So how else can we teach, share, and learn? By demonstrating it, by living it, by spending time in the Circle of who we are.

Some people don't have to question. A spoken truth rings true and they know it even if their intellect can't box it up neatly for them as a repeatable truism. It might just be a single phrase, like "Two Worlds ~ One Moment" ... and, if only for a second, they enter the flow. They don't really understand it with the mind, but something in them knows. Maybe their intellectual understanding slowly grows, trying to catch up to this *other knowing.* But they have moved back to the energy of *The Quest* and are no longer ruled by their questioning mind. They have moved closer to their earnest commitment to a path. You don't have to be seeking any kind of awakening or enlightenment. They can be a part of your quest but simply wanting

Earnest Commitment

peace is enough. Although the path to your true self is about being free of desires and fears, that one original desire for truth, compassion, authenticity, peace, and freedom must be there. Earnestly committing to these, as the most important things in your life, will invoke their power in every aspect of your life, in all your interests and loves.

You will thrive in life and have a foundation of peace even when there is pain. This is pain without suffering. If you live from the center of the Circle of who you are as a compassionate presence, everything you care about in life will benefit without sacrifice on your part. The best thing you can do for the whole world is to live at the center of the Circle of who you are.

I don't expect anyone to live this as I do. That is not what I mean. I live it this way because teaching, writing, and helping through this form is uniquely anchored into the *spine of my life* when I stand in the center of the Circle of who I am.

In the beginning, the Medicine of One may seem more like practicing and learning a path until it becomes how you move through life. There is no single way this is supposed to look from the outside. Practice has nothing to do with success and failure. There is no investment in an outcome. Just earnestly commit and do the best you can, which is different from one day, one month, one year ... One Moment to the next.

The magic happens through our earnest desire to live an awakened, authentic life and to follow the thread of the question, *Who am I* to its source. Nothing happens without this no matter which path you choose to walk. Your chosen path is a commitment to align with the spine of your life and live as the peace that you are. It is a commitment to be a compassionate presence that is given first to the life within you and then radiates out into the world effortlessly. Nothing happens unless it's so important that your very life depends on it. This commitment does not necessarily need a form with a name such as the *Medicine of One*. But most of us need a little help, a little guidance, and a little wisdom from those who have gone before us. The Medicine of One is one answer, one path to the Quiet One.

Know what you want ~ peace. Understand the path ~

Medicine of One

presence. Honor your uniqueness ~ spine of your life. Align it with your chosen path ~ be the demonstration. And then trust as the act of surrender to your greater self.

Chapter Twenty-Five

Courage and Patience

*I beg you, to have patience with everything unresolved
in your heart and to try to love the questions themselves
as if they were locked rooms or books written in a very
foreign language ... perhaps then, someday far in the
future, you will gradually, without even noticing it,
live your way into the answer.*
Letters to a Young Poet,
Rainer Maria Rilke,

Imagine you are going spelunking, caving, exploring subterranean caves. But you aren't just exploring, you are searching for something you lost. Now imagine a treasure you value, an heirloom given to you by your father who is now gone, has fallen down a hole in the earth that turns out to be a vast system of underground caverns. It is a round stone you wore on a cord around your neck and when the cord broke, the stone fell off and tumbled deep into the earth. Not only was this special stone passed down from your ancestors to give you an identity and a connection with them, and therefore a place in your family's history ... also it was believed to be endowed with magical powers. These powers had never manifested themselves in you, but you never gave up hoping they might. Because these powers could be used for the good of others and would make you feel your value in the world.

Now you stand before the only entrance to the maze

of caves. It's large enough for your body to slip into. You are about to embark on a journey to retrieve your identity, value, and power. Safety will also be involved because you must be keenly aware as you proceed to enter the dark unknown. You will have to invoke your courage, because caving is not something you know much about.

In you go, carrying enough food for a few days, wearing a helmet with a light to show the way ... with some extra batteries. Just moments after entering you wonder, *What the hell am I doing? This is crazy.* Unfortunately, the hole you crawl into on your belly is narrow and tilting downward. Gravity makes it impossible to reverse your motion. You have started your journey and the only choice is forward. For a few hours you lay there paralyzed with fear. Finally you know... *I have to move. I have to move forward hoping there is a way out.*

This is courage ... acting in spite of your fear. Courage does not listen to the voice of fear. Fear is there in the Circle of *you*. But you breathe, you relax, and you choose *forward* ... you choose *onward. Everything that you are lies in this forward.*

Two days later - an eternity - and you have found nothing. Even though you have moved forward courageously confronting your fear, weaving your way through the labyrinth of caves, you are completely lost and the last batteries in your helmet are beginning to die as the light fades.

Just at the moment the light is flickering, you come upon a large cavern where you can stand up. You see something on the wall and move closer to it. Some of it is difficult to make out because of water constantly dripping over it. But with the final light of your headlamp you read.

> *I searched and searched, defiantly ignoring my own safety. I hurried in this search because time was running out.*
>
> *Time ran out and here I am in this very spot where you stand.*
>
> *In my frenzy to find the truth, I burrowed deeply into the bowels of the earth.*
>
> *As darkness came, it seemed that the body scribbling these words would not survive.*

Courage and Patience

> .My mind badgered me and reeled with panic driven thoughts. It seemed that I had descended into hell on earth: my very own mind from which there was no exit. The walls themselves were my own hardened mind closing in on me.
>
> I kept following them. Rushing this way. Rushing that way. Believing this thought, then another counter thought, until I screamed for the quiet to save me!
>
> If you find no bones here, know that the unquenchable thirst of the human spirit for the absolute truth prevailed. The quiet came as I surrendered all my believing and believed in one thing only ~ I am this quiet.
>
> From my blossoming wisdom I urge you to surrender the courage that brought you here into the arms of infinite thoughtless patience. Let your courageous fire light the candle of patience and follow it forward. Let the light of your heart lead you back home. If you find no bones, I am home. My bones are home and home sings in my bones. Hear the singing of your true self in your bones. It's there ... just listen. Listen as the unity of courage and patience to this quiet of the true self that sings in your very bones.

Now the emptiness comes. But sitting in this emptiness you listen. You listen to your own breathing. You listen to your own heartbeat. You listen to the quiet, the penetrating, infinite quiet. Time disappears as the batteries die and the infinite darkness comes. In this still, quiet listening there is patience and strangely, peace. A voice speaks from inside, *I am the darkness listening.* You sit in the experience of the true meaning of this phrase. The fearful thought is there in the background like a stirring in this *darkness listening. Is this it, am I going to die?*

The need, which drove you to find the heirloom stone

of power, identity, and value are gone. It's as if it has disappeared. You can't find it in yourself. Your own quiet presence is so prominent that all the ideas of who you *thought you were*, what you *thought you needed,* which was *to be yourself,* have died. The question ... *Am I going to die* ... slides easily into ... *I have already died.* Even this thought you do not follow, because it is not an experience, only a concept. It is as if, when the batteries powering the light for your search faded, your fear-filled need for worth, value, and power faded with it. You are *nobody* with *no thought.*

Courageous, you sit as the *darkness listening*. Patiently, you do not move even as you hear a far away echo in your mind that says ... *I am trapped in the bowels of the earth. I am going to die*. You don't follow this thought either. You don't energize it. You can hear a counter voice urging you to push on ... *Get going or you are going to die!* You don't follow this thought either. You don't follow any of your thinking because the utter peace of yourself is everything you ever wanted. And you know this in your very bones. You are saturated with the *feeling of knowing* that is thoughtless. All assessments, statements of your *aha moments* and all counter statements of your physical predicament drift through the darkness that you are. You invest no energy in them. They are simply what they are ~ thoughts. You **are** *the darkness listening.*

I am the darkness *listening*. Understanding this sentence offers a great key. But understanding and the turning of the key happen through experiencing its mystery. Find a place to sit in pure darkness and let your eyes be ears and your ears be eyes. Fill the space all around with awareness that now has no object to fasten onto. This is why people feel impelled to close their eyes to find their peaceful self. It's important to be able to move beyond this.

I am the darkness *listening*. This means I am the presence that permeates the space where the sun of my world rises and sets, whether it rises in a world of chaos and turmoil or a world of calm and beauty. This *I* presence, which is my compassion and peace, is always there. It cannot go away. It's right there even in the darkest moments of life as your own unmoving peaceful presence. It's as close as your soft breath

Courage and Patience

and your soft relaxed body.

Now you know what it means to *give up believing in your thinking.* You see all these thoughts are just sitting there as worlds of possibilities. You contemplate: *Each of us has different history through which we interpret what we see before us, and what we project into the future. Every thought is just an opinion, every spoken word about this or that ... only opinions.* And then you break into uncontrollable laughter until you are *crying with laughter,* because even this thought is just that, a thought, and an opinion. One final smiling thought comes: *my own deep, eternal, aware silence is the only certain truth.*

Somehow it seems the darkness is lifting or being dissolved by your own quiet presence almost as if you are the sun itself coming to life out of nowhere. Dawn comes and you see you are sitting in the grandest of canyons, the walls of the canyon sing with tones of red and purple, sing with colors of bone white and orange brown. You see you are actually sitting in the middle of rapids, in a river, on a heart-shaped rock. The river moves, but you are motionless. You know yourself as being what the river flows through. You are that from which *the flow* is born. You *are.* That's all.

You walk as if carried on the wings of peace, out of the canyon, back into the world ... back into the world of death, war, violence, starvation, and destruction. But you walk through the world as the radiance of peace. And walking in this way is *the spine of your life.* Because you are free from your thinking, you are untouched, and you see only the great beauty ... first in yourself, then in everyone and in everything. You are not in a hurry to change the world or to save the world. Courageous and patient, you walk as radiant peace. And perhaps you meet others who have embarked on the journey that you *know.* You share your experience, your sense of truth, but as if energized from *the truth* and *the flow;* because there are truths of thought and speech birthed from the flow in the marriage of innocence and experience.

Even though you move through the world with a deep experiential knowing, you are above no one and you are walking the path. You live as the demonstration of what you know without proclaiming that you know anything. It takes courage to walk a path of awakening to truth, the courage of giving up identity. You have not emerged from your underworld journey of awakening as if to seize a new title of an "awakened one," because that would invoke separation between *who is awakened and who it is that is saying they are awakened.* There can only *be wakefulness.*

It takes great patience, and that patience is courageous because the strength must *patiently* balance itself with surrender and trust. It has to wait. The river is in no hurry to get to the sea. It just flows. It's really neither patient nor courageous. It just *is*. But the river doesn't think or have memory, because the river is just the flow. So the flow doesn't think, determine, or create. The flow is the first movement out of the void from which all creation springs. You do think, choose, and create. But you also doubt, fear, and desire, and these separate you from the flow. Courage and patience are necessary to re-enter the flow that carries you home.

When you are in pain, in that moment, painlessness is difficult to imagine. Knowing, or at least believing it will change, gives you the courageous faith to persist. Without true courage and patience, the unity of awareness, will, and trust cannot flower. Courage partners with will, and patience partners with trust. You can't have trust without patience, and you can't have courage without will.

The Circle is eternally patient because it's okay with what is there right now. Even if that *right now* is fear and resistance. When you align with the Circle of who you are, you immediately invoke your courage and your patience. Courage - because paradoxically it would be easier to stay with what you know and the way life has been, even if it is empty of life and love. Patience - because you are not in control and are willing to wait. There is no timetable and there is no idea of a final result that will endow the moment with acceptability.

Pleasure and pain are about what is acceptable and unacceptable. We desire what is acceptable and we fear what is unacceptable. Good health, abundance, love, friends, work that allows for the expression of the *spine of our life,* and living where we truly want to live are desirable and acceptable. Loneliness, struggle, disease, and pain, unfulfilling work, bore-

Courage and Patience

dom, feeling trapped where you live, these are undesirable and unacceptable. And we fear they won't change. But again, the desire and fear are greatly fueled by thinking, followed by believing that thinking.

Let's take pain, discomfort, and disease because they are very tangible and there's no mystery. We simply don't want them. Sometimes our bodies are living out a destiny that is irreversible. It is 39 years after my wild slide beneath the Healy. In spite of having done everything I possibly could, gravity working with the forces of natural aging continue to compromise the injured organism, primarily my spine. But as it continues, I continue with the intent of standing straight and lengthening my spine. Not with urgency but with courage and patience. To my *thinking mind* based on sensory feedback there has been little change, and in fact the experience can be interpreted by fear that things are worsening. A thought or feeling of futility can visit me but I let the *feeling of futility* move through me and do not get involved in the thought. Thought and feelings can enter our space. The mind likes to move. It's a choice of *believing* that lets them sweep us away into their world.

Even with a spin in your Circle that languishes in hopelessness, as long as you gently hold it as spacious compassion and let the feelings move, you will go on loving life and loving yourself. Once you start to stand in this commitment to being the Circle of compassion to yourself you cannot go backwards. Once you start to wake up, once you start to become aware and stop allowing your fear *to own you*, you can't back up, just like the descent into the caves, just like standing up straighter. Standing up straighter is a metaphor for standing in the truth of who you are. And that truth is still, peaceful, and quiet.

Paradoxically, as I move toward a straighter stance and alignment, the tissues in my neck pull down more vigorously, narrowing the space between the vertebra causing my skull to feel as if encased in a cement block. It feels like my body cannot keep up and change, and move back toward a healthy balance. It feels like that, but I don't buy into the thought that this is the truth. I continue as a spirit reaching, a tree fulfilling its destiny to embrace the sky. But because of courage and patience I reach from the stillness. I reach from the *now*. I reach from peace.

Gravity may continue its pull, but peace remains my truth. It is the truth of how I choose to walk through this life in which the acceptable and the unacceptable are constantly appearing. I reject nothing and believe nothing except that I will keep going without living for something to come later. I stand straight and tall in the acceptance of *now* ... and ... *I don't know*.

It takes great courage to ask and patiently love the question, "Who am I" and wait without rushing to answer it. It takes great courage to live the question as you patiently live your way into the answer. If you are reading this book you have made it this far. Take a breath and honor yourself for that. Believe in the feeling of that honor. Believe in its truth and allow that breath to bring you into being straight and tall in spirit, standing at the center of it all. Stand as the *stillness* to the unacceptable and the acceptable. Be who you are. Be the *Medicine of One*, your compassionate spacious presence. And in this standing you never stand alone.

Part Five

HOME

Medicine of One

Things had changed a lot in the last few years: things like walking to the tops of mountains, riding horses, chasing the dogs, sitting in the middle of the river just being quiet. For various reasons he wasn't able to get out to some of his sacred places as often. He tried to keep moving, but moving was getting more difficult since he had turned 107 years old. But it was okay because those hours of quiet out there in the vastness had accumulated within him. He still loved those places but it truly felt like they were a part of him now as he moved through his day. Even when he was forced to take a two or three hour nap with the dogs in the middle of the afternoon, he took a nap in the peace that he was, allowing his discomfort to be cradled in that peace.

From The Circle of Life
Lomakayu

Chapter Twenty-Six

The Quiet One

Here in this land are my sacred scriptures that speak to me in the language of silence. I sit here at the center of the Circle and give it all up to the Quiet One. Even my own personal quiet, I surrender.

The Medicine of One has grown from the very elemental forces of this land, a land of the greatest variety of landscapes, from vanilla scented Ponderosa Pine forest, to the drought resistant Mesquite, to the Piñon-Juniper woodlands, to the verdant paths of river and creeks ... rich with sycamore, cottonwood, walnut and hackberry and canyons of red, buff, white, orange and yellow. Cliffs, mountains, buttes, mesas, and pyramid-like cones thrust forth with the memories of ancient landscapes from oceans to floodplains, from sand dunes to lakes. Often when the wind blows it feels as if it's coming up off the ocean. And so it is for me, the *ocean of being ... the ocean of the One ...* a web of life where all that is unique in expression is resonant with the one ocean ... just as one drop of water has the whole ocean within it.

The Hopi and their ancestors have been the caretakers of this land a thousand years or more. The Hopi believe the earth was created when the *All Creator* was gazing at the earth from deep space, wondering what to do with it. He decided to send his helper *Spider Woman* there to set life in motion. When she arrived she scooped up two handfuls of earth and

Medicine of One

gifted her saliva into each hand. This saliva is the *life force*. This spit is water. Water is precious in these desert lands. From this action Pöqánghoya and Palöngawhoya, the two twin heroes, were birthed in her hands. Pöqánghoya went to the North Pole. He was the magician of shape, form, and structure, the web of life from which things emerge in *harmony and balance*. Palöngawhoya went to the South Pole. He was the *magician of music and vibration,* which resonates and energizes structure and form to give birth to life on the planet. Palöngawhoya went into deep meditation searching throughout the universe for the heartbeat of the Great Spirit. When he found it, he began to beat his drum, drawing that which gives movement and life to all things to the heart of the earth ... *the center*. At this *center* was a special crystalline rock that dispersed this life force to the surface of the earth where it gave birth to all life. Those places on the earth where the drumbeat is strongest are the sacred places, the doorways where the web of life can be entered and joined with ... where we, as a human expression of that original saliva of the divine, can return closer to home ... closer to the source ... closer to the great mystery.

I have many sacred places where this drumbeat speaks to me. My body of earth, water, air, and fire tells me where they are, not my mind. Over the course of many years, the more time I give to just being there, the more some strange magical *something* happens. It's as if some kind of mutual transmission of the *power of the One* is exchanged. I am infused and the place is infused without any effort from either one of us. After all, what more could the river or canyon do than just *be*? What more can I do? What greater gift can I give, than to just *be* ~ to just live at the center, as harmony and balance, allowing the force to move through my physical and spiritual spine and flowering outward as my unique heartfulness into the world?

The land is full of songs. It sings to me as a grand symphony in its vastness and every secret little place holds a melody, all born from the single harmonic of the Quiet One. It teaches me in its silent singing. It's not something I hear with my ears. It comes from listening with my heart, whose very

The Quiet One

rhythm beats in the harmonic ocean. My body is just a cup dipped in this ocean, dripping with tears of individuality. These gurus of the Southwest land of Arizona have been my greatest influences toward the birthing of this Medicine of One. But I also pay homage to all the wisdom teachings that have been birthed by that original saliva of the divine, sprung from this sacred web we are all part of; from Buddha to Ramana Maharshi, from the Aborigines of Australia to the Hopi and Navajo of the Southwest to mention only a few. I give thanks to their special gift that came into manifestation as the life force vibrated through the spine of their life. That spine is part of Pöqánghoya's gift of form, unique structure, and expression. The music of the spheres is Palöngawhoya's gift brought forth and delivered to the earth by his *deep listening.*

    I consider it a truth that there are places on this earth that carry a song that is in deep resonance to the song of who we are. There can be many of these places on the earth that carry the feeling of *home*. It feels like home and it helps carry us home to the *Self*.

    Many enlightened beings have been drawn to a single mountain, valley, or river where they never strayed, as if never straying from their deepest self. Part of the journey of the labyrinth is about arriving at that physical place as well. Often, as in my case, it has to wait until experience and exploration have completed themselves and your greatest commitment is to peace. Sometimes the choice of *home* is about the earthly family of friends and relatives. Whatever the choice, make sure that it is what allows you to have peace and live in the center of your truest *home of the heart*. And be patient, meeting your experiences fully as the flow rather than trying to willfully place that final piece at the center. If done willfully, it won't fit. And now, fittingly, I share my love song to Arizona:

> *You can see for miles and miles,*
> *North, South, West, East where earth meets sky*
> *You can see the ancient profiles*
> *In the ancestral clouds of the deep blue sky*
> *Land of Hopi, land of peaceful people*
> *Land of Navajo, Yavapai, people of the sun*

Medicine of One

Land of soaring stone, like church spires
Arizona land bequeath to sun

You can hear the singing sound of silence
You can smell the juniper all wet with rain
In the forests of ponderosa and painted deserts
It's a religion without a name

Arizona oh Arizona,
Land that speaks to our ancient hearts
Arizona oh Arizona,
Your nighttime skies full of breathing stars

When the sun comes up
Your skies sing with color
Sun goes down how can you not be a believer
I believe, I believe, I believe
In that sense of wonder
I believe, I believe, I believe,
I believe I'm a believer

Arizona oh Arizona,
Your saguaros sentinels in the desert so old
Arizona oh Arizona,
You are truly the seven cities of gold

I believe, I believe, I believe
In that sense of wonder
Oh I believe, I believe, I believe
In your lightening and thunder
Ah Aeya Aeya Aeya Aeya Oh
Gago Yawhani Nawah Heyah

Oh I believe, I believe, I believe
In that sense of wonder
Arizona, Oh Arizona

Arizona
by Lomakayu

The Quiet One

Desert Sky

In the desert, the fifth element of space is so powerfully present, and so the invitation to be spacious has immediacy. This loving spaciousness allows unrestrained movement of the air, of the earth, of the water, of the fiery sun in the sky. We are born from these five elements. And a combination of them prevails in every movement in this Circle of who we are as qualities. This is a *guru* that is vast, and in that vastness draws me into its resonance of unconditional *Oneness*. This blue-sky space is love. This endless sky is compassion ... compassion for all that moves within it ~ flocks of birds, solitary ravens, hawks, eagles, vultures, and clouds as subtle as a whiff of smoke to the dark foreboding ones, pregnant with torrential rains and arrows of lightening. Always moving ... always moving ... and yet the space itself is endless and unmoving.

The more I resonate with its vastness, with its limitlessness, with the infinity, the more I am the embodiment of this Medicine of One, the more loving I am to every movement within this Circle that I Am. Since I am this vastness when a strong wind blows in, *I* am not swept away like a leaf in a dust devil. But this may rightly express how one member of my Circle feels ~ overcome with the forces of life and living. And so there is the feeling of helplessness, of spinning, of being out of control. But *I* am the sky, and rather than panic and close the space with hard walled thoughts, I hold fast to my *Self* and let the *spin* spin itself out until calmness returns. From the spiraling dust devil the earth moves and spreads itself across the landscape in all the directions. Space to breathe allows movement.

My desert guru's teaching of Quiet vastness celebrates all the movements of life without being disturbed by them. Space cannot step out and detach from itself. So this detachment from the disturbance is fully engaged as a loving allowing of the wind, the rain, the sun, the moon, the stars, the earth, and all the creatures. It contains them like the mother's arms contain the whimpering infant in her embrace. This is not the detachment of someone discarding an emotional movement like a piece of clothing. It is a detachment that honors without judgment, for judgment is tight, closed, and stubbornly clings to *I know*. The spacious sky that you are knows only compassion.

We can feel trapped in our lives, in our daily habits and addictions, in our relationships and work, but the great suffering of imprisonment are the walls of our own mind. The movements of our own thoughts are like dust devils that pull us into them. How do you use your thoughts and silent words toward yourself? But most importantly, do you believe those thoughts? Do you take them on as the truth? How do you use your thoughts and the silent words you speak to yourself? We can't always control the movements of the mind. But you can choose what you believe. So know what you are choosing. The highest choice is to give very little credence to your thoughts, no matter what they say. Just let them be movements in this vast sky. This way you avoid self-deprecation or ego inflation. You avoid swinging from the opposites of right and wrong, success and failure, good and bad. They are like breezes and gusts of wind in the desert space; and you, always remembering that *you* are that space, that vast sky, that Medicine of One.

Guru Tree

The wonder ... the uniqueness ... the beauty of trees ... a barren land has its own song and magic of space and limitlessness. But the glory of a tree, and the glory of so many different kinds of trees ... how can I thank them all? All the trees I have known since I was a child, all the trees my child self climbed in and built tree houses in, sat in, and pondered the world from above? Trees scenting the air that I breathe, with the life of their subtle presence ... and the sound ... the sound ... from the rustling of aspen and cottonwoods to the skyward reaching redwoods, pines, spruce, and sequoias that sing with the sound of the ocean even though far inland away from the sea ... and the ancient alligator juniper and the wisdom of the oak tree. So many trees gifting me with smells, sounds, and the shade ... the cool shade breathing with their sound, scent, and the oxygenated breath of life.

When you look at the trees that lose their leaves in the wintertime it's like seeing the spine of their life. All the limbs are anchored into the main trunk of the tree. In that anchoring,

The Quiet One

all the way down into the ground, to the roots, is also the upward motion that reaches for the sky. Trees reach with great roots as if to the source below and they reach to the sky and source above. Like a two-tipped arrow they link the sky and the earth as a timeless eternal magic. They are a wondrous mirror of our own great connected **I**.

I have seen trees grow up through the middle of immense boulders and in their growth they find a way to the sky. I have seen trees whose roots became exposed by flooding and woven in amongst the roots were rocks, lovingly embraced. The rocks were not obstacles, they were now integrated and part of the tree's *treeness*. I have seen trees thrusting out sideways from steep cliffs and then angling up to the sky. I have seen trees on the hills above the ocean gracefully bending to the force of the wind but still expressing their uniqueness. I have seen trees whose limbs reached for the ground first before they angled to the sky, creating a beautiful *Spider Woman* form.

What starts as a seed in the ground thrusts upward into the world and is seen. No two trees are the alike, even if they are the same kind. Some, like Christmas trees, can seem very orderly and symmetrical in their expressive form. Some, like oaks, seem to meander and reach in forms that do not seem orderly. They all meet the forces of wind, water, and rock and find a balance and harmony. No two are the same and in their unique *treeness* is a gift of creative beauty ... an effortless gift that comes from just being.

One of my Circles is presided over by an old Utah juniper. You can sit and gaze straight out through the center of the Circle to a vast spectacle. Fifty feet below the Circle, junipers sketch the places where water flows downhill for miles, as if delineating the radiant song lines of the land. Buttes of white and red stand like *Holy Beings* in the distance. Finally, layer after layer of dark, wavy mountains fade into invisibility more than a hundred miles away. How lucky this old tree is to gaze on this vision at each morning's sunrise. How lucky I am to sit in the Circle in the shade of its *beingness* and let it teach me about *being*. I sit with my back on her peeling bark, a soft fibrous bark used by the ancient people that lived on this land as a kind of diaper in their *baby cradleboards*. And so she cradles me as I lean back and touch the teaching of ancient rootedness ... touch the teaching of silent presence ... transmitting our presence to one another ... and in that transmission we are not separate. No tree. No me. Just here. Two worlds ~ human and tree ~ One moment.

My *Guru Tree* invites me to pluck her green growth that smells so light and gentle with an aroma that brings calmness to the body. She invites me to pick her berries when ripe to heal the bladder and urinary system, another of her effortless gifts in just *being this juniper tree.* In this silent presence it's as if I am asked to give up the names of tree and juniper, and just be with another life on this planet that is born from the web of life, from the drumbeat of the life force. In that request I am asked to let go of all definitions of myself at the same time and just be quiet ... just be quiet to her compassionate shade ... to me, to birds, to insects, and to my dogs at my side. All are welcome ... the deer and the antelope, the mountain lion and the javelinas, the squirrels, mice, and chipmunks. All welcomed into her compassionate shade without rejection or judgment. My *Guru Tree of the Circle* teaches me the truth of effortless compassion.

All of these natural, effortless qualities emerge from the spine of this juniper tree's manifesting in this world. They are not tied to survival, although some of her natural effortless qualities can protect her from the invasion of insects and rodents. But there is no greed in her. She is the true demonstration of harmlessness.

River of Bone

There is a place of bone white rock that sings a song of silence and peace. It sings in my bones and lullabies my mind into its arms of harmonic quiet. A canyon where the river runs dry ... a wash where water seldom flows yet is formed by the flow of water ... white rock smoothed by water born sand. Water moves beneath the rock and sends its flowing magnetism to the surface. The water moves invisibly beneath the bones ... or through the bones. I feel it in my body ... like a dowser's wand to this living flow. This place is called Skeleton Bone. So here

The Quiet One

too is a current to surrender to. I bow to it as another of my gurus of the silence. I bow ... I listen ... I sit ... and I walk in its grace.

Our bones are full of space, far less solid than concrete, yet stronger, and they sing with the fire of electricity. They sing with the flow born from opposites, that spark of the life force as the One comes into form. Our bones are the deepest foundational structure of our body. Fish swim in the sea but they too have bones, and this place of bone white rock was originally sediment on the bottom of the ocean. When our bodies naturally return to the earth without the action of fire our bones survive, sometimes for many thousands of years, until they too become rock. Our bones sing with the songs of rock and stone. They channel through them an unnamable force. Many native healers pray to become a hollow bone in preparation to heal. Being a hollow bone is getting out of the way. It is an unobstructed channel through which the river of life can flow ... *through* me, not *by* me.

I come quietly and I sit. The longer I sit, the more I am permeated by the quiet that sleeps in my very bones. This place awakens me to what is within ... to the peace that I Am. All places help us to remember the quiet presence that we are. All places have their own unique song of this quiet ... some audible and some inaudible. They are all present as resonant gurus to carry us to our deeper truth.

Deep listening is not just with the ears and the eyes. This bone rock is silky smooth and cool in winter and pleasantly warm in summer. I lay in its warm white hand and surrender my tension, my history, my thinking, everything ... until the only thing left is this quiet feeling of *I Am*. In this I am physically touched by the rock, and resonantly touched as I surrender until nothing is left to surrender ... but something is still awake ... lying there.

All enlightenment techniques are meant to lead us to this quiet *I Amness* ... to taste it ... touch it ... hear it ... and to know it as the Oneness we seek ... that we all seek ... that we all are. In this surrendering of our history we become the presence that has been there in every moment and beyond the beginning and the end.

Medicine of One

But do you know what you seek? Or do you think you know and block the way to what is there in this so-called *knowing*. Can you touch the quiet in the rock? No matter where you live, even in the city there is rock, there is sky, there is sun, there is wind. Can you touch it with your deep listening? Or is there no time in your life to reclaim your deep listening this earth is willing to help you with?

People try to think their way to this *quiet* and it is this very thinking that must be given up. Give it up. This earth is here to help you give it up. But you must seek it out. You must go to it. You must surrender to it. Although I am sharing my special places of rock, when I say *earth*, I mean this earth we inhabit. This earth we sprout from is a living web that we are woven into. This web is home to the ocean, the mountains, the canyons, the forests, the lakes, the rivers, and the trees and rocks in your own backyard. The places that call to you could be on the sea, where you are held in a gentle breathing hand or sitting where water meets rock in a great crash and roar. The Medicine of One is my personal world, which I share with you. So take it and bring it into your own world in which you live. Don't defeat yourself with thoughts like *I don't have these kinds of places*. Find a way. Find a spot to be quiet. Don't wait.

You will find these white rocks in all of my Circles. It links them as one. I have never conceptualized this linking up of the Circles. It's something in the background of my awareness. These rocks, once they have been in a Circle, have the uncanny effect of balancing and strengthening people, of rooting them like an ancient tree. The strength of these rocks that have been in the Circle, I did not create or consciously orchestrate. I simply discovered it. I am always moving with the sense of *I don't know*, so that I may become aware of what may have always been there but never sensed before. And I will go on discovering as long as *I am Here.*

This sensing of the quiet deepens through the years. I seem to deepen into it. But it's just the tenacity of my mind giving way to a graceful fall ... into grace ... into the hands of the quiet godly Oneness. So many words to simply say, *Be Quiet. Be the Quiet.* So many words to make the journey to the true experience of what it means to be Bone Quiet ... as quiet as

The Quiet One

this canyon of boney, heavenly rock.

We start out following a rope trail of words, our minds grabbing the rope one hand after the other until we reach the chasm of no return. No thread of thought or word will carry us forward, no fiber of what we know. We have to leap into the quiet space and trust. We have to act. We must begin the journey back to the center of who we are.

The River Breathes

The River breathes and I breathe. I am the River. Because the River is something that seems to be in constant motion, and therefore the creator of many wondrous musical sounds, it's easy to get caught in the spell of its song and miss the deeper quiet magic that has no beginning, end, or middle. Most rivers from the eagle's eye seemingly appear to have a beginning and an end. But they, too, are a Circle of life and are a Holy Being of presence.

The River is a strong contrast to this spacious empty land around it and yet, as all of my other teachers, its ultimate teaching is this silent presence from which all the parts emerge from its flow.

For many years now I have stood like a heron in the water, sat still like a rabbit in the grass, and walked its shores like a lion, naked as any of the creatures that inhabit that world of The River. In that pure, sensorial, bodily experience where nothing separates me from the sun, the wind, the rock, and the water the way home to who I Am is easily found. The feeling of being present is dynamic, but my body and its pleasurable feelings are but another resident of the River. The question is *what is it that inhabits it all from beginning to end? Who inhabits the bodily presence known as me?* When I touch the river's being, I touch my own being. The two are inseparable. And so, the river, in its presence reflects this deepest teaching back to me, and the River sees itself. I Am the River. The River breathes and I breathe.

But let me explore some more profound teachings expressed through the life that moves in the river with the only tool I have to speak to you from this page ~ words. And let me speak in the present as I have just returned from the River.

Medicine of One

The leaves have been falling from the trees along the River. There are sycamore, cottonwood, alder, ash, hackberry, willow, juniper ... ah, all these beautiful names we give things. Each has a unique leaf, or foliage, a shape that determines how the wind carries them in their fall to the ground, or in their journey down the River. I was watching a long slender willow leaf move beneath the surface in the current of the River. That current is like touching the being of the River in its prime movement. The leaf is swept along and the unique shape of the leaf affects the quality of its movement and its speed, as well as where it gets stuck. If that leaf had a mind that was trying to navigate the River, in other words, to think its way along based on what it saw down River and what it was anticipating, it might act as we often do and become fearful and try to control its experience to avoid some future outcome. Much of what that leaf *thought* it saw would be based on its experience back upstream from where it began. It seems the more experience it has, the more it thinks. And so, it begins to separate itself from the current and resist the flow, trying to second-guess, often times ending up in disaster, whereas if it had just relaxed and surrendered to the current it would have found its way home safely.

Each of us is like a different shaped leaf, riding the River of life. We are all very unique, no two exactly alike. Like those leaves, no two will be carried along in exactly the same way. So even in surrender, their unique expression is inevitable. For the surrender in this human form is not just to that universal current, but also to our unique manifestations, and that is a surrender that can also be called trust ~ thus the cliché ... *going with the flow.*

Today the River calls me. I see the dance of light on the water moving in places yet smooth as glass, churning here, foaming there, swirling ... all the movements of life in a Oneness called the River. This River is me ... these movements are reflections of movements within me. It teaches me to let it all move and be the *River presence* to it all.

The surface of the River is always moving and changing. The movement of water over the Riverbed of our history creates this dance, this dream. Silt, sand, dirt can color the wa-

The Quiet One

ter, or in their absence the water is a mirror. Rocks and boulders stir the water and disturb the surface, like our own history, churning the waters. From the beginning to the end of the River there is one thing that remains unbroken and undisturbed ~ the current, like the life force itself. This current is born from the surrender of the water to the earth. Water flows from above to below. This current is not unlike the I that is born as you too emerge from above to below, journeying through the birth canal into your first breath and into the formation of a personality/character whose primary objective becomes to defend itself. This ego forgets its source as the current and identifies with the disturbance. It defends that separation and becomes more separate. The mind is the surface of the River. The truth of who you are is the current. Go to the River ... sit and join with the current ... with the quiet and the unbroken Oneness.

Everything teaches me. Here are my scriptures turning me to the quiet love of life, which as the quiet has no quality, not even the quality of love. Love, too, is an idea. The Circle is an idea. The Medicine of One is an idea, until you step into it, like stepping into the River. Water, is an idea, until you touch it, then a sensorial experience of wetness is experienced. Who is this that feels the wetness? What is here as this *me?* These are the questions that return me to the quiet that is the answer.

The cold mud between my toes ... the birds in winter trees ... the pulse of my heart ... a rhythm rhyming with the life force of my breath ... and this I born from the dance of the elements. The River breathes and I breathe. I am the River. I am the *flow*.

Holy Being of the Wind

When the wind blows it sings as it flows over the land. When it blows through cottonwoods its song is different than the song it creates when it blows high above in the tops of ponderosa pine. Together wind and trees make music. The earth is the instrument and the wind is like the breath of the flute player. The body of earth, too, is like a wonderful flute. We are here to let the Great Spirit come singing through us, each with our own wonderful song. No two flutes are alike. There may be a limited amount of notes, yet as composers have demonstrated from the inception of their art since the beginning of time, those notes can come together in an infinite number of ways. Just like people, the wood, the stone, even the plastic of the flute can come from so many different places on the earth. Eastern cedar is not the same as western cedar. Walnut has a different resonance than birch. You will get more resonance from a wood flute than a stone flute. Soft woods have the most resonance. So like the flute, be soft toward yourself and free your music ... and resonate with harmony as compassion and peace.

As people, it is better to be soft with a strong resonance so our song can travel past the limitations of who we think we are and ripple through the world. We harden to protect ourselves. Hardening can start in the mind with a thought or belief, and then it finds its way into the body.

This wondrous instrument known as *the body* is a doorway to the soul. Let the wind invite you, with your breath, to lovingly soften to the forgotten sacred within that you have come to fear. We fear our own feelings, our own music. We seem to harden to the world, but this hardening is to our most intimate and deep pain, which becomes a wall to that true presence we are. The breath of the wind teaches the soft touch of love even when it's strong. But the wind, too, can reflect any emotional movement even in its power of destruction as in the rage of a tornado or a hurricane.

The holes of the flute are like centers in the body that get gummed up with old trauma and pain. We get out of harmony and our song seems to leave us. Or, the channel through which the spirit of one moves gets tied in a series of knots that becomes a pattern of protection. These knots are woven from the fabric of thoughts and beliefs, and the elemental substance of emotions. The Soul Dreaming session I do is an untying of these knots so the beauty of our song sings forth. When your soul's song can fly like an uncaged bird, you become the wind and the hawk or the raven, the eagle, or the vulture upon the wind, and there is only the song of creation.

The wind is different when I am below in a canyon

The Quiet One

than it is when I am on a mountaintop, above. Cool, hot, gentle, strong, scented with juniper, creosote or the very earth itself. We hear it. We see it. We smell it. We feel it. We touch its being with our being. It's an invitation.

The wind is a gentle or strong presence that can seem to respond to a feeling, or a thought or an action. When you sit in the Circle as this *true action of self-love* and the feelings ripple through you as you kneel with your head to the ground, the touch of the wind breathes with a song of liberation.

As if what moves inside of you is moving all around you, it can bless you and grace you as the touch of the quiet presence that moves all things. The spiraling tracks on the tips of your fingers and the top of your head for the Navajo are reflections of this great mystery of movement that is in all life.

You breathe, the trees breathe and the very ground breathes, and the wind connects you with the breathing movement in all things. So even in its motion it can carry you to the motionless beginning, to the motionless quiet that you are. The wind is not only something you hear but also something you feel. The wind on your whole body can anchor you in the *now*. All you have to do is reengage your *deep listening*.

The phrase, *Take me to where the wind begins,* is like asking your inner guru to take you to where your thinking begins, to the presence that it all emerges from. *Take me to where the wind begins. Take me to the center from which all things stir.*

Is there any place on the earth where the wind does not blow? This is a presence you can find in the tallest building and the largest city on the earth. Just stick your head out the window. Or go up on top of the roof and ask, "Take me to where the wind begins." Even in deep tunnels and caverns in the earth the air moves. There are holes in the earth on the Colorado Plateau where the air rushes out at 30 miles per hour and rushes back in at the same speed, set in motion by underground waters that ebb and flow with the moon. The Hopi believe these are the very lungs of the earth. So even this physical earth breathes.

What if you are some place where the wind does not blow? Then don't give up. This wind is the call of the quiet and the quiet has many doors. The true and ultimate door is closer than anything else in the world ~ You. As long as you inhabit this physical form, the wind is moving within you.

Does the wind know me? Does it talk to me? *Take me to where the wind begins*, I ask. Where does it begin? Where does it start? Let the place where the wind begins be a mystery. You can explain it through weather science, but you cannot pin point where it begins. You cannot pin point where it ends. You feel it when it moves and you feel it when it stops. It is a mystery, this place of origin. But if you ask, it's as if you can go there. But it's the same kind of *there* as the place where your thinking begins. As you sit feeling where the wind begins, feel it come together with the place where your thinking begins. You can't name it. *Take me to where the wind begins* is another mantra/chant that echoes *I don't know.* You can only feel it as a keenly awake presence that is at once the whole sky, with you as the center, a center that then becomes centerless and One.

You don't have to think about breathing. It just happens. But what has accumulated as unmoved emotional history weighs upon you. The willingness to breathe is the willingness to live and feel. Most thinking interrupts full deep natural breathing, because most thinking is about controlling. This is why your breath is so important to this Medicine Of One. It's immediate and tangible and you can free it. You can *clear the way* to full body breathing. You can breathe beyond the limits of your body as the Circle and your breath can be filled with the *true action of love*. You only have to allow it and have faith. Let your very breath be a love that you give to yourself. Let the wind be your very breath circling back to you as a blessing. Let it bless you as you abide in the place where *the wind begins.*

Circle of Sun

Perhaps my greatest guru is the very sun itself. The sun was there before life on this planet, and as man inhabited the earth it probably became the first projection from the mind of *God*. It mirrors the quiet warm radiance that *I Am*. By the river, in the stone, barefoot in the desert or sitting in the Circle, the sun is always there, leading me to its warm mystery of brilliant presence. With effortless ease, it brings me home if I simply stop in my tracks and receive its constant blessing. As the cottonwood tree roots seek out the life giving water, their green tear drop leaves cry with fluttering joy and stretch to the sky in worship. With a touch of rain in the summer and the sudden heat of the sun, the sage and grasses, the juniper and creosote gift the air with the smell of their odiferous blood. The desert is the place of the sun.

No wonder this orb in the sky unites the beginnings of all earth's creative evolution. The Great Father of us all making love to this Great Mother of an earth for a million millennia of loved filled dawns and sunsets. Through its daily presence I am tied to the primordial *I Am.*

There is nothing to do but mirror it ... nothing. All movement requires an expenditure of energy. Thoughts are movements, and the smallest thought is still an effort. To simply abide in the effortless warmth of the sun as the warmth of the self, to surrender to this is to not even lift the smallest finger movement of the mind's constantly shaping hands that somehow want to fidget endlessly. In this *no-movement* the illusion of control is a truth instantly realized.

So the sun is the elemental fire of the desert. It is a radiant life force that mirrors the radiant presence born from the food of my body. I receive its grace with the deepest gratitude. I come to the sun naked as the day I was born, before I was given a name, before I was trained in the ways of social behavior, before I spoke or even knew there existed *I, you, me, them,* and even *we.* Yes, I go to this sun each day to remember who I really am. When it's cloudy do I feel its golden warming absence? Of course, but it's just a reminder, an ever-present teaching that the true sun of my being is never absent no matter what is going on in my life. The sun is just another one of my guru teachers always referring me back to the source that I Am.

Walk in Beauty
My very own feet guide me into the quiet and deliver me to the peace of the earth. The soles of my feet are ears that

listen without thought. Too long without walking barefoot in the desert or along the river, and something in me craves this touch of grace that speaks from the earth through my soles to my soul.

In the winter the rocks along the river are too cold to give voice, but sometimes, several weeks after it has rained, the desert earth, having frozen and then dried in this expanded state, becomes soft and spongy. Places you could not tread, because of the sharpness of small stones and the twigs of plants, now invite you into this barefooted, sensuous mystery of airy earth. But still I tread softly as if speaking to the earth ... as if lovingly treading on my own being.

I walk with nothing between the elements and me, enjoying the wonder of this sensorial experience that my physical body brings me. One of the reasons I walk about in the wilderness without the barrier of clothing is that it enhances the experience of n*o-separation*. But if you can use that heightened feeling as a beacon, guiding you home to this **I** that is present to the experience and then let it go, then just let the body have its experience. Stay grounded in that which was there, present for every experience, even beyond what is often called the *observer*. Let go of this *observing* and literally allow this **I** to melt into the eternally inseparable.

If you can't walk as I do, walk with clothing that is light and pleasant with shoes that invite the feeling of bare feet. I walk grounded as the presence that is aware of the many modes of sensing. I still get to delight in this world of the five elements and the senses. Just because I know the absolute truth of who I am is before and beyond my actual birth and death in this world, does not mean that I cannot take pleasure in the physicality of being here.

This is some of the unspoken spirituality of the aboriginal. This stalking of the quiet, even as a hunter, brings you into the Oneness of the wind and the sun, the earth and the very moisture in your mouth. Nothing moves in your mind and everything speaks. Even the ordinary act of urinating seems to be part of this continuum. You are alert without any tension. You are the bow readied as if waiting, but waiting for nothing because the target is you.

The Quiet One

When it's hot in the summer the multicolored rock beds along the river heat up. Large rocks massage your feet differently than small rocks, and the warm pressure as you carefully bounce from one rock to another is an unmatched reflexology. By midday, the dark rocks are too hot to walk on, and so your feet must seek out the white, light colored rocks. You must give full attention to the moment. Then the shore turns to a lush green ... cool, damp ... interrupted every now and then by a warm slab of volcanic basalt. The momentary hotness is welcomed, followed shortly by the wet blades of grass.

This sensorial experience can be enjoyed and supportive. You do not have to abstain from the physicality of the human experience. Bring your pain to the land and let it help you. Let the earth hold you as you give up holding this **i**-*dentity* together.

Finally, I stand in the river, sometimes in the sand, sometimes in the mud ... and sometimes on river-cooled rocks slippery with algae. The river breathes and my feet breathe. These feet of mine in dialogue with the earth have carried me into the arms of my grace. What is me is brought forth and sings in my bones through this dialogue and connection. Gently, my **i**-*dentity* that is linked to stories of pain is dissolved, as I let the earth hold me and deliver me into the truth of *Who Am I*.

The Quiet One of the Circle

So many places, so many songs, so many forms of the quiet, and yet *One silent presence* as I commune with the earth. This quiet is the very pulsing heart of the Medicine Of One. It is the deepest teaching of this earth. Only I must choose to remember and in this remembrance I am home.

Here in this land are my sacred scriptures that speak to me in the language of silence. I sit here at the center of the Circle and give it all up to the Quiet One. Even my own personal quiet, I surrender.

The Circle is always there, for the Circle lives within me. I am this Circle of presence. But these sacred Circles in the desert make it easier to not be distracted by the demands of everyday life. I step into them naked of all identity, the same as the rock I sit upon. I sit with the finger of my mind pointing at my own presence ... the feeling of it ... and something in me lets go ... allowing something deeper to rise to the surface. It's like a sigh of absolute trust that settles me down, fills me as a compassionate presence, and I am at rest on the foundation of all that is.

Always remember you are the Circle. You are the Quiet One that the tears, the rage, and the terror move in. And you are the Circle that momentary happiness, creative thinking, falling in love and passionate drive move in. You are the Quiet One that the mind moves within, whether they are thoughts that soar to the greatest heights or tumble to the great lows. Into this compassionate presence invite all your fears, hopes, worries and all your dreams, laughter, joy. As this Circle, as that Quiet One, you are peace and bliss and nothing is thrown out of the Circle of your love.

Let the gurus of the earth teach you, whether it's a tree, the ocean, a mountain, a river, a canyon, a butterfly or a bird. Abide in the oneness you share with life. While you dwell in an elemental body as an individual creation of the One, be alive and live. Be willing to be the whole world, and love this world of your humanity. The earth teaches us how to engage our own pain and pleasure. As a guru it reflects to me who I really am and teaches me how to engage the beauty and the death of life. She breathes and allows, whether it's a still mirror of water reflecting a golden sunset or an earthquake sending a giant wave of destruction toward the shoreline.

"Support, touch and embrace all that moves within you as the *unconditionally loving mother* as I, the earth, support you," she whispers to us. "In this living at the center, you are the effortless receiving and giving of compassion and love that is *freedom.*"

Other than living from this center place, I give up all ideas about my *self* as the doer of anything. It is done and it gets done, and what is done is done without my interference.

The spine of my life is open to the flow. The unique, creative will is the hollow bone called Loma Kayu. Even this *me* as a thinking entity is sourced not from **i**-*dentity* but from the **i**-*lessness*. The very words of this book are authored

The Quiet One

through Lomakayu ... not *by* Lomakayu ... so let the signature at the end simply be:

Everything Finished Well

Medicine of One

Tribute
Anne, *Sister of Many Lives*

Long before the Circle there was my brother, Lomakayu, stepping in to guide me to a better place, and to help me learn to love and accept myself. I have assisted him in his Circles, been guided by him to my own discarded undesirable detritus, and inspired to embrace my own Circle at home. I have watched him follow this path of Medicine of One in his own life. So yes, I am his sister, but I'm also someone like you who has been able to find my way back to my true self because of his guidance and example.

We have all had trauma in our lives. Events, which caused us pain, made our spirits shrink, damaged our delicate sense of self-acceptance, and changed us in other unknown ways ... from our birth selves to the person we *think* we are right now. Some of us remain diminished, while others leap forward into battle whenever they perceive something is a threat. We can be full of rage, fear, and a sense of being overwhelmed ... or full of emptiness. But is this who we really are? Absolutely not. Our stories take over and mold us. They keep us in various forms of self-imprisonment.

If you have opened the pages of this book and *breathe*d in the words ... if you make a sincere commitment to be present and walk the path of Medicine of One ... you will find yourself in your own Circle of loving compassion and self acceptance ... you will find you have compassion for what you have denied, felt threatened by or attempted to toss out of your Circle.

I made this commitment. I hope you make one also.

Medicine of One

Glossary

Big I: ... transcends our stories and serves the greater you that inevitably serves the greater whole of the world. The big **I** joins heaven and earth. The mind turned inward to the little **i** is the big **I**, the self.

Circle: ... the feeling of soft, relaxed, spacious breathing, and an unthinking presence, which are like the sky that everything moves in; a living form of your own spacious, big heartedness to all that moves within you.

Clear the Way: ... is to melt down through the frozen pain with the very warmth of self-love. It is the heartfelt reentering into the unlived and the unloved experiences within ourselves, a conscious flight into the dark forgotten rejected pain as a compassionate liberating light. Clearing the way is like breaking a part of yourself out of prison with compassion. It's an act of liberation. To be free of all history, all stories.

Deep Listening: ... the *listening,* which is your *beingness*; profound attentiveness. It is this *listening* that brings you the experience which answers the question ... *Who am I?* Awareness that hears what emerges from the flow and experiences the connectedness before it separates into events of the material world.

Flow: ... Listening to the ground of your being brings you into relationship with Holy *Being* so you may *go with the flow*. *Flow* is moving through the world of duality connected to that ONE that you are. *Flow* is a great trust in a *knowing prior to thought, prior to what you believe.* It is from the sense of *flow* and listening that a trusting faith can come. To enter this *flow* is to give up being the *doer* who accomplishes and the thinker who knows.

Gathering Soul Medicine: ... is to gather all manner of physical objects to give form to any aspect of their story and helps people to move out of their analytical mind into their *feeling* body and truly engage the energies of their feelings; consciously choosing to bring back into the Circle the rejected, abandoned, and imprisoned emotional forces in their soul's history that still remain unintegrated.

Hungry Ghost: ... something inside of us hungering for the essentials of life and who we are and is created through the deprivation of one's basic needs; the hunger for the feeling of identity and value that is bestowed upon us through loving recognition. When it's absent we intensely seek this value from outside ourselves.

Identity: ... identity is a thing of thought, belief, memory, and mind turned outward to the world of objects: the hardened idea of who we *think* we are.

Little i: ... when you establish *who you are* in the action of thinking, your experience is a world of many voices; the voice of the warrior who defends by attacking with hard confidence and tough courage; the voice of the victim who fears worries, and doubts; and the voice of shame, guilt, and self-blame that undermines true worth. These voices are many and when you root yourself in them you live in a world of confusion and separation. These are the spins in the Circle of who you really are. In their spinning they think endlessly. This is what I mean by the little **i** with the spinning dot that is a head.

Magic: ... inexplicable appearances in this tangible world that emerge from the flow that we allow to touch us and speak to us with wonder and awe.

Medicine of One: ... is the path of self-love and compassion, a godly love that is the Circle and uses the Circle to understand that path.

Messengers of Synchronicity: ... anything that comes into your awareness that rings with a resonance, which makes you stop, pause, and breathe in the magic.

Path: ... something you commit yourself to living everyday as a way of life. Walking the path frees the flow of the spine of your life; how you live in the flow and allow it to flow through you and through the spine of your life.

Primordial Movements: ... physical gesture and voice, the perfect *feeling form,* words, tone, and volume that if entered and surrendered to, will liberate the imprisoned life within; these can, in an instant, bridge the world of opposites that have been separated

Soul Medicine: ... speaks to you in the language of the soul through the energies of symbolism, metaphor, synchronicity, and the sheer poetry of life. This language emerges from the flow; stirs whatever needs to move for freedom and peace; anything that creates a bridge for your awareness to cross and allows you to embrace your deep, soulful being with the compassion of the Circle; helps us to come back into balance and harmony so we can align with the *spine of our life* ~ our gift and the thrust of why we are here on the earth.

Soul: ... something unique, enlivened with life force, shaped by experience; the soul is an experiential energy that ripples inseparably out into the greater Circle of you. The soul comes from *One Light* into this world and manifests as a *soul rainbow* that is the unique blue print of a living form.

Spin: ... A movement, a force, and a spin in your Circle that would have you mistake it for your *self.*

Spine of Your Life: ... the life force that comes through form and expressively thrusts itself into the world; the potential of a unique human being

To Be the Circle: ... *To be the Circle* is a journey to the truth of who you are as you clear the way to your deep listening, and enter the flow that carries you home; to be who you are; to expand with your breath as a life-giving God of your world and then to expand with the mind beyond the very

Medicine of One

breadth of who *you think* you are; to give up being anchored in believing your thinking and *be* the loving space in which everything moves; to love your own imperfections and your reactions to others' behavior; to be uninvolved in your thinking.

True Action of Self-Love: ... is beyond the thought or concept of love. It is the breath of the Circle that touches fear as the cradling arms of a mother's unconditional love; your presence as a focused compassion to all emotional movements.

Index

Affectionate, 9, 54, 68
Affectionate Awareness, 9, 54, 68
Arizona, viii-ix, xii, 15, 57, 59, 225
Arizona,
    song, 131, 203-204
Awakened Ones, 98
Beat poetry, 159
Beauty, iv, xv, 26, 61, 75, 113, 116, 132, 137-8, 143, 148, 157, 194-5, 206-7, 214, 218, 220
    dog, 153, 154, 225
Behavior, x, 9-14, 40, 50-1, 80, 86, 97, 99, 161, 176, 217
Being trapped, 79-82
Beingness, 23-4, 26-7, 42, 63, 126, 157, 164, 207
    Holy, 138
Believing your thinking, 38, 174
Berkeley, 59, 185
Be the Circle, iv, xiv, 16, 18, 20, 39, 54, 56, 68, 72, 91, 101, 104, 146, 173-7, 179, 181-3
Believing your thinking, 38, 174
Big I, 17, 19, 25, 37, 43, 53, 88-9, 104, 126-7, 139, 169-70, 174
Bii'istíín, 137
Black Mountains, 41
Blue Mountain Flat on Top, 15, 41

Buddha, 169, 188, 203
Buttes, 16, 30, 201, 207
California, 47-8, 59, 70
Centeredness, 18, 44
Central America, 58
Chasta, 117
Cheyenne, 66-7, 108-12, 118-9, 132-3, 152
Character, 25, 93, 106, 117, 161-2, 213
Chief Joseph, 98, 169
China, 87
    Sea, 59
Christ, 12, 98, 169, 188
Circle,
    lives within us, xii, 15, 20
    making a, 16-20
    of compassion, 40, 74, 79, 82, 92, 102, 127, 139, 148, 169, 182, 197
    of Sun, 217
    of who you are, 19, 33, 58, 100, 114, 128, 150-1, 171, 181, 189, 196
    of you, 4, 11, 17, 19, 24, 27, 33, 38, 50, 84, 89, 100, 122, 124, 192
    Sacred, 22, 74, 122, 146, 149, 220
    stone, 18
    The Circle of Life, 2, 56, 116, 166, 200
Circumpunct, 18
Clear the way, iii, ix, x, 29,

32-3, 42, 50, 53, 56, 60, 82, 129-30, 148, 173-4, 178-9
Coffee Gallery, 160
Colorado Plateau, 15, 57, 215
Coming home, xi, 59, 158, 163
Commitment, iv-v, 6, 42, 69, 177, 181-2, 185-6, 188-9, 197, 203, 223, 226
Control,
  loss of, 80
  protector controller, 37, 66
Courage, iv, vii, 22, 29, 32, 33, 35, 43, 147, 151, 169, 191-8
Creation, viii, 18, 63, 72, 106, 134, 137, 157, 196, 215, 220
Creative force, 24, 157, 159, 164
Creativity, iii, 150, 155-9, 161, 163-4
Dante's *Divine Comedy*, 160
Dark nothing, 106, 113
Darkness listening, 193-4, 197
Deep listening, iii, 36, 41-5, 56. 62, 89, 91, 103, 137, 173-5, 186, 203, 209-10, 215,
Depression, 97-8
Dowsing stick, 20
Durrell, Lawrence, 186
Echinacea, 109
Emotions

trapped emotions, 37
emotional energy, 37, 50, 94, 103, 179
unmoved, 60. 65, 81, 162, 175
polarities, 100
Empty, xiv, 5, 10, 73-7, 87-8, 96, 106, 112, 121, 132, 155, 196, 211
Emptiness, xiv, 86-7, 107-108, 112, 193, 223
Enlightened,
  beings, 203
  Ones, 73, 126
  teachings, 73
Eternal Moment, 103
Experience,
  meeting experience, 29
  unified, 93-4
Faith, iii, xiii-xiv, 40, 74, 131-2, 139-40, 164, 196, 216
False center, 44
False thread, 44
Far East, 59, 87
Fault, 181
Flow, 137-41
  go with the, 137-8
  ride the flow, 30
Forgiveness, 20, 151
Four Corners, 118
Fragile, 36, 40, 66, 68, 80, 88-9, 96, 102, 104
Fragileness, 80, 126, 170
Freedom, iii, ix, xi, 11, 25, 32-4, 53, 61, 68, 79, 82, 84, 114, 123, 126, 144-5, 148, 150-1, 183, 189, 220

Frozen, ix, 4, 32, 52, 57, 72, 75, 93, 146, 218
  frozen moments, 20, 60
Futility, 197
Gandhi, 26, 169
Gathering Soul Medicine, 145
Genet, Jean, 186
Geronimo, 94-5
Ginsberg, Allen, 159
Great Father, 217
Great Mother, 217
Great Mystery, 115, 122, 157, 163
Great Spirit, 32-3. 202-214
Grief, ix, 10, 75-6, 84, 96, 107, 110, 146
Grounded, 95, 128, 138, 147, 218
  being grounded, 58
  ungrounded, 52, 58
Guardian of the heart, 114
Guilt, 11, 35, 50-1
Guru,
  desert, 205
  tree, iv, 206, 208
  within, 6, 177
Harmlessness, iv, 72, 167-170, 182, 208
Hanta Yo, 32, 76, 108-9, 112, 132-3, 151-2
Harmony, 24, 31, 58, 94, 100, 102, 134, 144-5, 149, 155, 181, 184, 202, 207, 214
Hate, 80, 100
Hawaiian Islands, 58
Heightened Awareness, 83
Helplessness, 40, 54, 80, 89, 95-6, 98-9, 101-2, 117, 132, 205
Hereness, 27, 30, 64, 88-9 134-5, 178, 182
Hippies, 160
Hollow bone, 209, 221
Holy Being of the Wind, 132, 137, 213
Hopi, xix, 15, 57-9, 94, 156, 167, 191-2, 201, 203, 215
Hungry ghost, iii, 44, 85-9, 97, 99, 170, 187
Identity, x, xiv, 5, 11-13, 17, 37, 51-2, 65, 87-9, 95, 124, 160, 182, 191-192, 194, 196, 220
Immobilization, 81, 95, 98,
Imprisonment, 80, 206, 223
Japan, 87
Jerome, 15, 18
Joplin, Janis, 160
Judgment, 6, 10-11, 16, 20, 36, 49, 54, 64, 72, 123-124, 126, 134, 169-71, 177, 191, 205, 208
Kachina, 15, 116
Karma, 11
Kaufman, Bobby, 159
Kerouac, Jack, 159
Knowing,
  instinctive knowing, 38
  feeling of, 194
Labyrinth, xv-xvi, 37, 42-4, 58-62, 86, 114, 125, 158, 192, 203
Liberation, 32, 51, 64, 100, 102, 156, 174-5, 215
Limitations, 21, 84, 214

Listening,
  be the, 140
darkness listening, 193,194
  deep listening, iii, 36, 41-5, 56, 62, 89, 91, 103, 137, 173-175, 187, 203, 209-10, 215
Little i, 17, 25, 35, 37, 43, 52-3, 86, 88-9, 114, 126-7, 129, 134, 139, 167-8, 170, 174, 182
Loneliness, 99,197
Los Angeles, 59, 162
Losses, 5, 75, 105, 108, 111, 113
Love,
  I want to be, 44, 74, 169
  soft love of the warrior, 70-1
  unconditional, 16, 32, 67, 86
Maasaw, 58
Mandela, Nelson, 26, 79, 98, 169
Magic, xi, 30, 37, 42, 76, 100, 116, 138, 143-4, 147, 149, 151-4, 161, 163-4, 189, 191, 202, 206-7, 211
  of soul medicine, iii, 143
Magnet, 154
  Magnetic, 16, 97, 140
  Magnetize, 60-1, 99, 154
Maharshi, Ramana, 126, 188, 203
Manipulation, 10, 12
Maze, xvi, 43-4, 60, 86, 89, 91, 95, 97, 114, 173, 192
Merchant Marine, 85
Mesas, 16, 201
Migrations, 57, 59, 163
Mingus Mountain, 15, 133
Mystery, 19, 20, 30, 33, 64, 72, 134, 140, 144, 147, 155, 168, 170, 183-4, 194, 202, 215-8, 227
  of you, 140, 144
Navajo, xix, 17, 137, 203-4, 215
New York City, 19, 59, 162, 185
Niłch'i Diyin, 137
North Beach, 159-60
O'Neil, Eugene, 186
One that I am, 72, 131
Oneness, xi, 4, 19-20, 30, 32, 37, 42, 53, 84, 125, 134, 144, 205, 209, 210, 212-13, 219-20
Opposites, 36, 94, 100-2, 125, 139, 147, 177, 206, 209
Oraibi, 58
Osha, 109, 118-19
Palöngawhoya, 57, 202-3
Panama Canal, 59
Path of the Circle, 15, 129, 166, 188
Path of Self-Inquiry, *126*
Patience, ix, 130, 191, 193, 196-8
Perpetrator, 68, 93, 95, 97-98
Philadelphia, 59
Physical body, 81, 113, 218

Poles, North and South, 94, 202
Polarize, 52, 60, 89, 91-2, 94, 98-9, 114, 124
Pöqánghoya, 57, 202-3
Powerlessness, 40, 54, 80, 89, 93, 95-6, 98, 101-2, 169-170, 183
Prayer, 74, 77, 122, 131-5, 164
Primordial movements, 147
Prison, ix, xii, 4, 6, 13, 32, 50, 73, 79-84, 91, 96, 114, 186
Protector controller, 37, 66
Psychological gesture, 97, 99
Pyramids, 16
Quest, viii, ix, 108, 129, 157-8, 161-2, 185, 189, 208
Questioning, 109, 148, 186-188
Quiet,
  be the, 17, 20, 176, 179-210
  personal, 17, 220-1
  greater, 17
Quiet One, iv, xv, xvi, 19, 38, 131, 155, 177, 190, 201-2, 219, 220
  Holy presence of the, 131
  of the Circle, iv, 219
Rage, ix, 50-1, 54, 72, 93-6, 100, 109, 130, 147, 214
Ram Dass, 127

Religion, xix, 12, 16, 51, 131, 167, 170, 204
Resistance, 52, 137, 196
Richfield, Utah, 47
Right,
  being right, 35, 40, 120, 125, 139
  righteous, 10, 52, 81, 95, 101, 112
River,
  I am the, xv, 211, 213
  breathes, iv, x, xv, 211, 213, 219
  of bone, 208
Sacred Circle, 20, 22, 74, 122, 146, 149, 220
Sacred places, 4, 137, 200, 202
Saint Francis, 169
Saloon, The, 160
San Francisco, 15, 59, 158-60, 162
Santa Cruz Mountains, 47, 70
Self,
  acceptance, 223
  compassion, 3, 6, 9, 11, 12, 14, 18, 26, 32-3, 53, 79, 81, 84, 89, 92-3, 101, 145
  hate, 11
  healing, 101
Shadow, 37, 49-54, 148
Shepard, Sam, 186
Sign Language, 97, 102
Skeleton Bone, 16, 173, 208
Socrates, 117
Soul Dreaming, xvi, 50,

100, 118, 162, 214, 226
Soul loss, 98
Soul magic, 144
Soul Medicine, iii, 62, 139, 143-5, 148-9, 154
Soul rainbow, 30
Spaciousness, 15, 72, 84, 113, 114, 178
Spider Woman, 201, 207
Spins, xii, 35, 37, 53, 65, 99, 170, 174, 182
  spinning, xvii, 35, 37, 42, 52, 60, 72, 91, 129, 168, 205
  spins of emotions, 65
Spine of your life, iii, xiv, 14, 21, 23-5, 27, 33, 61, 103, 124, 150-1, 163, 182, 184-5, 189-90, 195
  greater spine, 27
Spirituality, iii, xix, 52, 89, 218
Stream of consciousness, 159
Suffering, 62, 71-4, 77, 80-2, 99, 114, 117, 120, 124, 127-9, 150, 158, 160, 181, 186, 189, 206
Sun that you are, 14
Sundance, 225
Survivalist mind, xvi, 62, 98
Symbols, xiii, xiv, 18-9
Synchronicity, 144
  messengers of, 144
Taos, 59

Terror, 93-4, 96, 100-02, 125, 146, 177, 220
Theater, 158, 161-2, 185
Thoreau, Henry David, 161
Threat, 12, 23, 36, 38, 42, 66, 69-70, 80-81, 88-92, 98, 130, 159, 176, 223.
Transformation, 62, 101, 105, 110, 126, 147, 162,
Trapped, 31, 37, 39, 49, 50, 52, 54, 79-83, 95-8, 113-4, 141, 148-9, 154, 175, 194, 197, 204
Trauma, 5, 25, 48, 52, 58, 66, 89, 93-4, 106, 138, 148, 150, 214, 223
Treeness, 207
Trigger, xv, 88
True action of self-love, iii, 68
Truth that you are, 14, 117, 122
Two worlds ~ One Moment, 5, 151, 158, 188, 208
Verde Valley, 15, 41, 225
Vesuvio's, 159
Vision Quest, 108, 226
Voices, 35, 38, 44, 65-6, 68, 69
Williams, Tennessee, 186
Where the wind begins, 215-6
Yavapai, xix, 14, 204

About the Author:

Clay Lomakayu lives in the Verde Valley near Sedona, Arizona with his dogs, Beauty and Sundance, who are also his devoted helpers. He is a soul dreamer in the shamanic tradition and the originator of primordial movement, an intuitive body based technique for aiding emotional movements of the soul. Together with his canine assistants, he has been guiding, teaching, and assisting people to heal and come home to themselves for 25 years. *Medicine of One* is the result of working with thousands of clients from all over the world.

Medicine of One

Contact and Resources
Visit Website: www.medicineofone.com
Email: lomakayu@medicineofone.com

VIDEOS
There are videos that correspond with each of the chapters in this book to aid and enhance your understanding. They can be found on Lomakayu's website
www.medicineofone.com

SERVICES
Shamanic Healing and Counseling
Spiritual Retreats
Vision Quests
Soul Dreaming
Commitment Ceremonies

The mystery in me honors the mystery in you ... blessed be.
Lomakayu

Made in the
USA
Lexington, KY